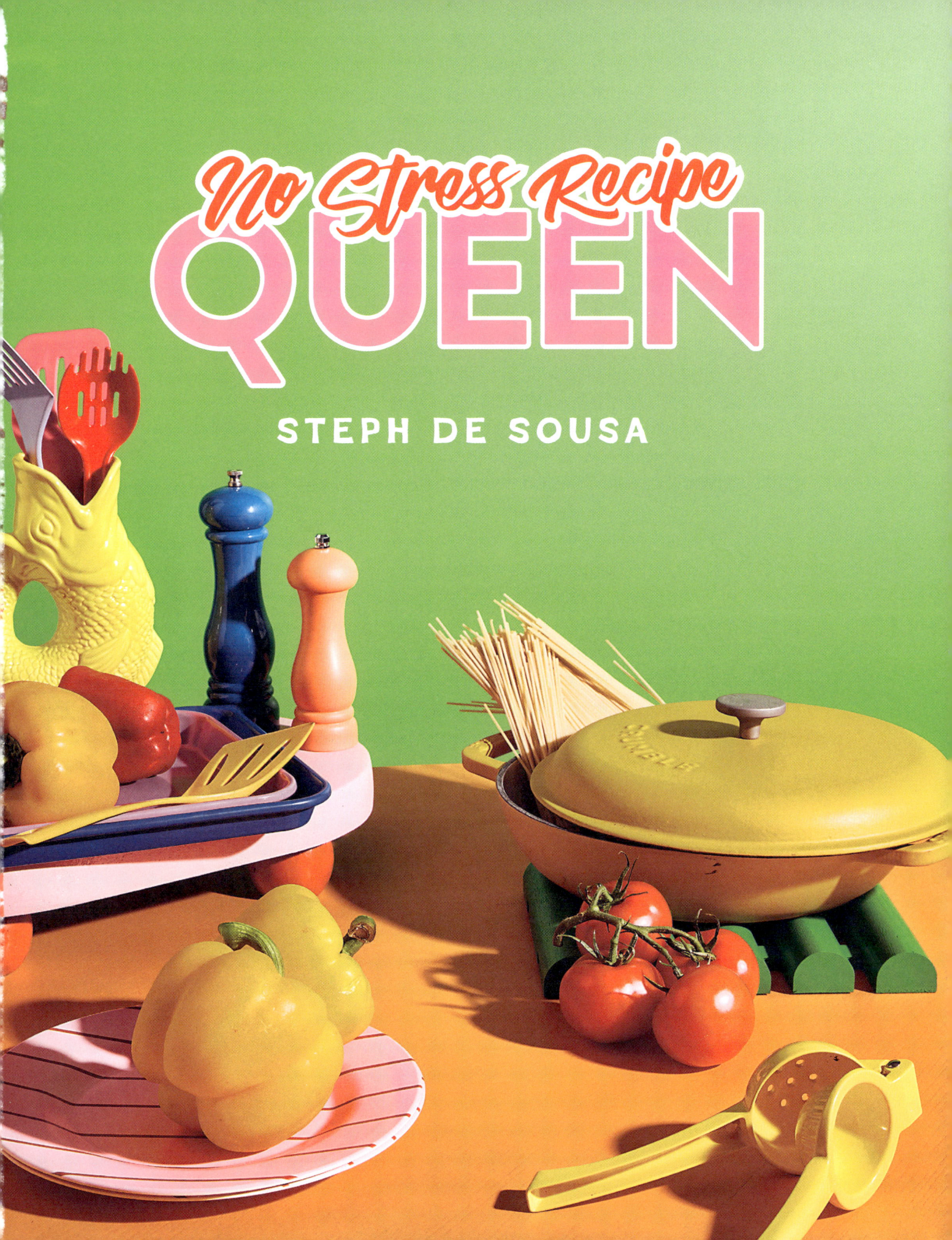

STEPH DE SOUSA

To my family – the official taste-testers, dish-washers and my forever cheer squad. Without you, this is impossible.

And to every busy cook who's ever stood in the kitchen wondering, 'What's for dinner?' – this one's for you.

♥ Steph

HarperCollinsPublishers

CONTENTS

NO STRESS COOKING BASICS 6

FAST & FAB 9

Weeknight chaos is sorted. These speedy dinners are on the table in 30 minutes or less – no stress, just fab food fast. Perfect for hungry mouths and zero patience.

SET & FORGET 35

Let your oven, slow cooker or air fryer do the hard work. These hands-off meals are made for busy days, long to-do lists, and anyone who wants dinner to cook itself.

COOK ONCE, FEAST TWICE 65

Double-duty dinners that save your sanity. These big-batch beauties give you tonight's dinner and tomorrow's freezer stash. Less effort, more eating.

EASY WEEKEND WOW 87

Laid-back cooking that still brings the wow. These are the recipes for when you've got a little more time, want to treat your family or invite friends over, and still keep things simple.

SWEET & SIMPLE 107

Desserts that deliver without the drama. These easy treats are big on comfort and low on effort – think quick puddings, no-fuss bakes and sweet little wins for any night of the week.

NO STRESS PANTRY ESSENTIALS 124

CONVERSION CHART 125

INDEX 126

NO STRESS COOKING BASICS

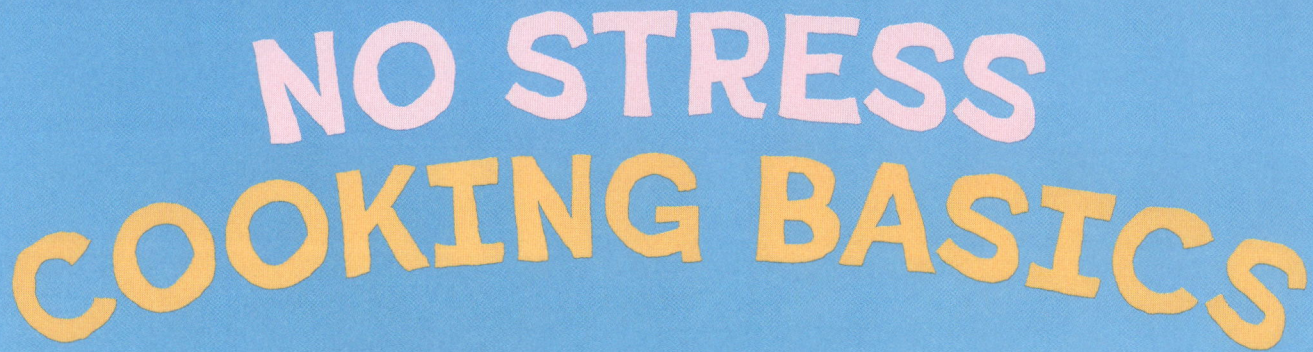

No stress cooking is all about keeping things simple, fun and fuss-free. You don't need fancy skills, tricky techniques or a pantry full of exotic ingredients to make delicious food.

With a few basic tricks up your sleeve and easy recipes that actually work, you'll be whipping up dinners that taste amazing without breaking a sweat.

Think one-pan wonders, quick flavour boosters and clever shortcuts – because dinner should feel doable, not stressful.

COOKING PERFECT PASTA EVERY TIME

Bring a large pan of salted water to the boil, add your pasta and stir, so it doesn't stick. Cook for 1–2 minutes less than the packet says, then taste – you want it tender with a little bite. Scoop out ¼ cup pasta water before draining, to add to your sauce to make it silky.

HOW TO SAUTÉ ONIONS LIKE A PRO

Heat a pan, drizzle in a little oil, toss in your onions and add a pinch of salt. Let them sizzle without stirring too much until soft and slightly golden – this takes 5–8 minutes. Don't rush it, this step adds magic flavour to everything!

THE SECRET TO CRISPY MINCE

To avoid grey mush, stop stirring! When cooking mince, break it up and let it sit in the pan undisturbed until it turns brown and crispy underneath. Then flip and repeat for golden nuggets of flavour.

YOUR GO-TO SALAD DRESSING

Shake together: ¼ cup olive oil, 1 tbsp vinegar (or lemon juice), 1 tsp Dijon mustard (or honey), and a pinch of salt and pepper. Done! Use on salad, drizzle over grilled veggies or even roast chicken.

NO-FAIL STOVETOP OR MICROWAVE RICE

For perfect fluffy rice: put 1 cup rice, 1½ cups stock, 1 tsp salt and 1 tbsp oil in a small pan. Bring to a boil, pop the lid on, and simmer on low for 12 minutes or microwave, covered, on HIGH for 15 minutes. Set aside, covered, for 5 minutes. Don't peek – it needs the steam to finish cooking!

FAST & FLAVOUR-PACKED STIR-FRY SAUCE

Mix together: 2 tbsp soy sauce, 1 tbsp oyster sauce, 1 tsp sugar and 1 tsp cornflour with ¼ cup water. Add it to your cooked meat and veggies, let it bubble and thicken slightly … and boom!

CRACKING THE CREAMY FACTOR

Cream cheese, sour cream, or even a splash of pasta water can help make a sauce glossy and rich. Don't stress about exact amounts, just gradually add, stir and taste for wow.

FREEZER MAGIC: COOL IT FAST

If you're batch cooking, spread your food out in a shallow container and let it cool before popping in the freezer. Label it and add a date! That way, future you knows exactly what's for dinner and when it was made.

THE LAZY ROAST VEGGIE TRICK

Chop any veggie (carrot, pumpkin, sweet potato, onion, etc.), drizzle with oil, season with salt and pepper, then roast in a hot oven at 220°C or air fryer at 200°C until golden and crispy. Done. Perfect with everything.

CHICKEN STOCK HACK

Keep a jar of stock powder in your pantry; it's your secret flavour weapon. Mix together: 1 tbsp chicken stock and 1 cup hot water. Use for soups, sauces, stir-fries, or to cook rice with extra flavour.

FAST & FAB
—

Weeknight chaos is sorted. These speedy dinners are on the table in 30 minutes or less – no stress, just fab food fast. Perfect for hungry mouths and zero patience.

STEPH SAYS

GOES GREAT WITH JACKET POTATOES OR WRAPPED IN WARM FLATBREAD WITH A QUICK SALAD. JUST REMOVE THE MEAT FROM THE BONES AND SLICE BEFORE WRAPPING.

SIZZLE & DRIZZLE LAMB CHOPS SOUVLAKI-STYLE

SERVES 4

These juicy, lemony chops with creamy garlicky yoghurt are like a mini-Greek holiday on your plate. It's a dinner that feels a bit fancy but really takes no effort – just a quick marinade, a hot air fryer and boom – dinner is done.

WHAT YOU NEED

- 2 TBSP OLIVE OIL
- 2 TBSP CRUSHED GARLIC
- 1 TBSP DRIED OREGANO
- 2 TSP SALT
- JUICE OF 1½ LEMONS
- 6 LAMB LOIN CHOPS
- TO SERVE: LEMON WEDGES, LETTUCE, MINT AND CUCUMBER

FOR THE GARLICKY YOGHURT

- 1 CUP GREEK YOGHURT
- 1 CLOVE GARLIC, CRUSHED
- 2 TBSP CHOPPED MINT
- 1 TSP SALT
- JUICE OF ½ LEMON

WHAT YOU DO

In a large bowl, pop the olive oil, garlic, oregano, salt and lemon juice and give it a good whisk. Add your chops and give them a massage so they're covered in all that garlicky, herby goodness. If you've got time, let them marinate for 30 minutes or refrigerate for up to a day. If not, don't worry, they will still be yum!

Preheat your air fryer to 200°C. Pop the chops into the basket in a single layer and set the timer for 10 minutes, flipping halfway through. Check to see if they are how you like them, juicy or golden brown! For more golden chops, reset the timer for a further 2 minutes.

While they're cooking, in a small bowl, stir together all the garlicky yoghurt ingredients.

Serve your chops hot with a generous dollop of yoghurt sauce, lemon wedges, lettuce, mint and cucumber.

PREP & COOK TIME
20 mins

SERVES 4

A big bowl of golden curried noodles packed with juicy pork, crunchy veggies and tender little prawns? Yes please! These fakeaway favourite Singapore noodles come together in one pan with a whole lotta flavour and not a lotta fuss.

GOLDEN NOODLE STIR-UP

WHAT YOU NEED

- 200G DRIED RICE VERMICELLI NOODLES
- 2 EGGS
- OLIVE OIL, TO DRIZZLE
- 500G PORK MINCE
- 1 SMALL ONION, THINLY SLICED
- 250G PKT COLESLAW MIX
- 1 TBSP CRUSHED GARLIC
- 1 TBSP CURRY POWDER
- 2 TSP FISH SAUCE
- ¼ CUP SOY SAUCE
- ¼ CUP CHINESE COOKING WINE
- 1 TSP SUGAR
- 200G CAN BABY PRAWNS, DRAINED
- TO SERVE: SLICED GREEN ONION AND SLICED RED CHILLI

WHAT YOU DO

Soften the vermicelli noodles following the packet instructions, drain, then pop them aside for later.

Crack the eggs into a bowl and give them a quick whisk. Heat a drizzle of oil in a large pan or wok over medium heat. Add eggs and stir until just scrambled. Then, remove and set aside.

In the same pan, add the pork mince and break it up with a spoon. Let it sit in the pan without stirring for a few minutes until it's nice and golden. Next, throw in the sliced onion and coleslaw mix. Stir-fry for a few minutes until they start to soften.

Now, it's spice time! Add the crushed garlic, curry powder, fish sauce, soy sauce, Chinese cooking wine and sugar. Give it all a good mix and cook for 2 minutes, so the flavours can mingle.

Add the prawns, scrambled eggs and soaked noodles to the pan. Grab some salad servers and give everything a good toss. Once, everything is mixed and coated in golden sauce, top with green onions and chilli, dish it up and slurp away – it's better than takeaway!

PREP & COOK TIME
20 mins

STEPH SAYS

THIS SAUCE WORKS A TREAT WITH BEEF, CHICKEN, OR RICOTTA AND SPINACH RAVIOLI.

RAVIOLI WITH TOMATO AND BASIL MAGIC

SERVES 4

I affectionately call this my 'can't be arsed pasta dinner'. It's rich, saucy, and packed with flavour – plus the spinach and basil make you feel like you've totally nailed the whole 'greens with dinner' thing. You can use any ravioli you like, and it all comes together faster than you can say 'pass the parmesan!'

WHAT YOU NEED

1 PKT RAVIOLI (APPROX 630G)

700G JAR TOMATO PASSATA

½ CUP RED WINE OR WATER

1 TBSP CHICKEN STOCK POWDER

1 TSP CASTER SUGAR

1 TSP SALT

PINCH OF PEPPER

300G BABY SPINACH LEAVES

1 BUNCH BASIL LEAVES

1 CUP MIXED OLIVES (OPTIONAL)

SPLASH OF CREAM (OPTIONAL)

TO SERVE: GRATED PARMESAN

WHAT YOU DO

Bring a large pan of water to the boil and cook the ravioli following the packet instructions.

Now, while that's bubbling away, grab a pan and pour in the passata and wine, then sprinkle in the stock powder, sugar, salt and pepper. Let it simmer over medium heat for 5 minutes.

Toss in your spinach leaves, basil leaves and olives. Once the ravioli is cooked, drain and pop straight into the pan with your tomato basil magic sauce.

Now is when you can add a splash of cream if you like a rosy, pink sauce. Give everything a gentle stir until the spinach wilts and the sauce hugs every ravioli piece.

Scoop into bowls and finish with a flurry of grated parmesan on top.

PREP & COOK TIME
25 mins

SERVES 4

This comforting and nourishing curry is like a warm tropical hug in a bowl. It's light, fragrant and loaded with good stuff. Juicy cherry tomatoes, snappy green beans and buttery barramundi, all swirled in a creamy, spiced coconut sauce. It's the kind of dinner that tastes fancy but is secretly super simple.

ONE-PAN COCONUT CURRY FISH DELIGHT

WHAT YOU NEED

- OLIVE OIL, TO DRIZZLE
- 1 ONION, SLICED
- 1 TBSP CRUSHED GINGER
- 1 TBSP CURRY POWDER
- 1 TBSP GARAM MASALA
- 1 TSP CHILLI POWDER (OPTIONAL)
- 1 TBSP CHICKEN STOCK POWDER
- 400G CAN COCONUT MILK
- 200G CHERRY TOMATOES
- 300G GREEN BEANS, HALVED
- 500G DICED BARRAMUNDI
- 1 LIME
- SALT AND PEPPER

WHAT YOU DO

Heat a drizzle of oil in a large pan over medium-high heat. Add the onions and cook for 3 minutes until they soften up and smell sweet. Stir in the ginger, curry powder, garam masala, chilli powder and stock powder. Stir it all around for 1 minute to wake everything up.

Pour the coconut milk into the pan, tumble in the cherry tomatoes and add 1 cup water. Give everything a good stir. Once it starts bubbling, turn the heat to medium and let it simmer away for 5 minutes.

Now, add the beans and fish, give it a gentle stir. Cook uncovered for another 5 minutes until the fish is just cooked and the beans are still a little crunchy.

Once everything is cooked to perfection, squeeze the juice of the lime over the top. Season with salt and pepper. Now, you're ready to serve!

PREP & COOK TIME
35 mins

STEPH SAYS

SERVE SPOONED OVER FLUFFY STEAMED RICE AND DIG IN.

STEPH SAYS

SERVE IT WITH 400G CHERRY TRUSS TOMATOES, LIGHTLY GRILLED UNTIL JUST BLISTERED.

SERVES 4

This one-pan wonder is what weeknight dreams are made of! Juicy chicken, tubular pasta, creamy cheese, and a big hit of pesto all cooked up in one large, cosy pot. It's quick, it's easy, and it tastes like something you'd order at a fancy café – but you made it in your pyjamas. Let's do it.

GREEN GOODNESS MAC ATTACK

WHAT YOU NEED

OLIVE OIL, TO DRIZZLE

500G CHICKEN THIGH FILLETS

1 TBSP CRUSHED GARLIC

2 TBSP CHICKEN STOCK POWDER

250G MACARONI

250G PKT CREAM CHEESE

190G JAR BASIL PESTO

300G BABY SPINACH LEAVES

1 CUP GRATED PARMESAN

JUICE OF 1 LEMON

TO SERVE: HANDFUL OF BASIL (OPTIONAL)

WHAT YOU DO

Heat a drizzle of oil in a large pan over medium-high heat. Then, pop your chicken into the hot pan. Cook 4 minutes each side or until lightly golden and it starts to smell delicious. Add the garlic and stock powder and give it all a happy little stir for 1 minute.

Pour in 1-litre boiling water and add the macaroni. Stir it through, then turn the heat down and let it bubble away gently for 8 minutes or until the pasta is just cooked.

Now for the fun bit! Plonk in your cream cheese and pesto. Stir, stir, stir until everything melts into a sea of creamy goodness.

Scatter in the spinach and half the parmesan. Stir until the spinach is wilted and everything looks like a big green cheesy hug.

Finish it off with lemon juice, taste it, and add a pinch of salt and pepper if you think it needs it. Nearly there, just scoop it into bowls, sprinkle with the basil and remaining parmesan, and devour it while it's hot and melty.

PREP & COOK TIME
35 mins

SERVES 4

Some nights you need dinner *yesterday* – this is one of those beauties that saves the day. It's fast, full of flavour, and uses things you've probably already got in the fridge or freezer. Best bit? It all comes together in one large sizzling pan. Let's get it done!

MINCE MAGIC RICE BOWL

WHAT YOU NEED

4 EGGS

OLIVE OIL, TO DRIZZLE

500G BEEF MINCE

2 CUPS FROZEN PEAS, CARROT AND CORN

1 TBSP CRUSHED GARLIC

1 TBSP CRUSHED GINGER

¼ CUP SOY SAUCE

2 TBSP OYSTER SAUCE

2 X 250G PKT MICROWAVE RICE

4 GREEN ONIONS, SLICED

WHAT YOU DO

Crack your eggs into a bowl and whisk them up like you mean it. Heat a drizzle of oil in a wok or large frying pan over high heat. Add the eggs, stir until scrambled and just cooked. Scoop them out and set aside.

Add your beef mince to the hot pan, and break it up a bit with a spoon, then don't touch it – let it sizzle until crispy and golden underneath. Once your beef's looking tasty, toss in your frozen veggies, garlic, ginger, soy sauce and oyster sauce. Give it a large stir and let everything heat up for 2–3 minutes.

Open the packets of rice and dump over the mince in the pan – no need to microwave first. Stir it all around until the rice is nicely mixed through and hot. Return the eggs back to the pan with the green onions and give it one last magic toss.

Scoop into bowls and if you like things spicy, add a splash of chilli oil or fresh chopped chilli for a fiery kick.

PREP & COOK TIME
20 mins

STEPH SAYS

IF YOU LIKE A LITTLE FIRE, DRIZZLE WITH CHILLI OIL.

SERVES 4

If you're craving something warm, fragrant, and full of slurpy goodness – this quick laksa is your go to. It's a big comforting bowl of spicy coconut soup with juicy prawns, crunchy veggies, and noodles that soak up *all* the flavour. It's ready in a flash to slurp up and feel the joy.

LAKSA THAT LOVES YOU BACK

WHAT YOU NEED

250G NOODLES (ANY KIND YOU LOVE)

2 TBSP OLIVE OIL

¼ CUP LAKSA PASTE OR THAI RED CURRY PASTE

400ML CAN COCONUT MILK

2L CHICKEN STOCK

250G SNOW PEAS

3 BULBS BOK CHOY

500G FROZEN PEELED GREEN PRAWNS

2 CUPS FRIED TOFU PUFFS (OPTIONAL)

2 TBSP FISH SAUCE

JUICE OF 1 LIME

2 CUPS BEAN SPROUTS

3 SLICED GREEN ONIONS

WHAT YOU DO

Cook the noodles following the packet instructions, drain, then set aside.

Place a large pan over medium heat and add the olive oil and curry paste. Let it sizzle and bubble away for 2 minutes to wake up the flavours. Pour in the coconut milk and chicken stock and give it a stir. While that's heating up, top and tail your snow peas and separate your bok choy into leaves.

When the soup starts bubbling, add the prawns to the pan, along with the snow peas, bok choy and tofu puffs. Bring to a simmer, then cook for just 2 more magic minutes – your prawns will be perfectly pink.

Turn off the heat, add the fish sauce, lime juice and crunchy bean sprouts. Pop your noodles into bowls, then ladle the steamy, fragrant laksa right over the top. Finish with a sprinkle of green onions.

PREP & COOK TIME
20 mins

SERVES 4

Need a zippy, zingy dinner in minutes? This one's a total weeknight wonder! Juicy steak, crunchy veggies and a sweet-salty dressing that's bursting with flavour. It's fresh, fast and absolutely fabulous – perfect for when you want something that *looks* fancy but takes barely any effort. Let's do it!

FAST & SASSY THAI BEEF NOODLE SALAD

WHAT YOU NEED

100G DRIED RICE VERMICELLI NOODLES

OLIVE OIL, TO DRIZZLE

4 SIZZLE STEAKS

200G CHERRY TOMATOES, HALVED

250G BABY CUCUMBERS, SLICED INTO RIBBONS

½ RED ONION, THINLY SLICED

300G MIXED LEAVES

1 CUP MINT LEAVES

1 CUP CORIANDER LEAVES

1 CUP SALTED PEANUTS

FOR THE THAI DRESSING

JUICE OF 2 LIMES

2 TBSP FISH SAUCE

¼ CUP SWEET CHILLI SAUCE

2 TBSP BROWN SUGAR

WHAT YOU DO

Soften the noodles following the packet instruction, drain and set them aside.

Heat a drizzle of oil in large pan over medium heat. Add the steaks to your hot pan and sizzle for 1–2 minutes or until cooked just how you like them. Set aside on a plate to rest for 5 minutes, then once rested, slice into bite-sized strips.

This gives you plenty of time to get started on the salad dressing action: in a large salad bowl, stir together your dressing ingredients until it's all smooth. Toss in the noodles, tomato, cucumber, red onion, mixed leaves, mint, coriander and peanuts. Give everything a gentle toss to coat in that sweet-tangy dressing. Then, lay your juicy steak slices over the top like a salad crown.

PREP & COOK TIME

30 mins

STEPH SAYS

IF YOU LIKE IT SPICY, FEEL FREE TO THROW IN A FEW FRESH CHILLI SLICES TOO!

STEPH SAYS

IF YOU'RE FEELING FANCY, ADD A HANDFUL OF CORIANDER LEAVES.

SERVES 4

This speedy stir-fry is your midweek dinner dream! Juicy pork, crunchy veggies, slurpy noodles, and a sticky ginger-honey sauce all come together in a flash. It's a delicious excuse to skip takeaway, and trust me, once you try that zingy sauce, you'll want to pour it on everything!

SAUCY PORK & NOODLE SLURP-UP

WHAT YOU NEED

OLIVE OIL, TO DRIZZLE

500G WHOLE PORK FILLET, THINLY SLICED

400G PKT STIR-FRY VEGETABLES

1 RED CAPSICUM, SLICED

450G HOKKIEN NOODLES

FOR THE ZINGY SAUCE

1 TBSP CRUSHED GINGER

¼ CUP HONEY

¼ CUP LIGHT SOY SAUCE

JUICE OF 1 LIME

1 TBSP CHICKEN STOCK POWDER

1 TSP CORNFLOUR

WHAT YOU DO

First, let's get cracking on the zingy sauce. Pop all your sauce ingredients in a bowl and give them a good whisk. Then, set aside for later.

Heat a drizzle of oil in large pan or wok over medium heat until hot. Toss in your pork slices and let them sizzle until they brown and cook through.

Add in your stir-fry veggies and red capsicum and give it all a good mix. Cook for 3 minutes until they start to soften but still have a little crunch. Pour in the zingy sauce and stir it all around until everything is glossy and the sauce thickens. Turn off the heat.

Pop your noodles in a microwave-safe bowl and cook for 2 minutes or until steamy and ready to slurp.

Divide the steaming noodles between your bowls and top with the saucy pork and veggies. Dinner's done!

PREP & COOK TIME
25 mins

SANG CHOI BAU WOW!

SERVES 4

This weeknight winner of crunchy lettuce cups stuffed with sticky-sweet pork and crunchy toppings is messy, fresh and fun to eat! And you don't even need to plate it up, simply pop everything in the middle of the table and let everyone build their own sang choi bau.

WHAT YOU NEED

- OLIVE OIL, TO DRIZZLE
- 500G PORK MINCE
- 1 ONION, DICED
- 1 TSP CRUSHED GARLIC
- 1 TSP CRUSHED GINGER
- 300G PKT COLESLAW MIX
- 2 CUPS BEAN SPROUTS
- 1 SMALL COS LETTUCE

FOR THE SANG CHOI BAU SAUCE

- 1 TSP WHITE WINE VINEGAR
- 2 TBSP OYSTER SAUCE
- 2 TBSP KECAP MANIS
- 2 TBSP SOY SAUCE
- 1 TBSP CASTER SUGAR

TO SERVE

- 1 LIME, CUT INTO WEDGES
- 1 CUP CRISPY NOODLES
- 1 CUP ROASTED PEANUTS
- SLICED GREEN ONION
- SLICED RED CHILLI

WHAT YOU DO

First let's make the sang choi bau sauce. In a small bowl, mix the sauce ingredients and set aside.

Heat a drizzle of oil in a frying pan or wok until smoking hot. Toss in the pork mince and break it up with a spoon. Don't fuss with it – let it sit in the pan and sizzle away until golden and crispy underneath. Once the pork is brown and delish, give it a final stir.

Toss in the onion, garlic and ginger, stir-fry for 2 minutes or until the kitchen smells amazing. Pour in the sang choi bau sauce and throw in the coleslaw mix and bean sprouts. Stir everything together and cook just until the coleslaw starts to soften – don't let it go soggy! Turn off the heat.

Now for the fun bit – separate the iceberg lettuce into whole leaves. These are your crunchy little edible bowls for filling.

Pop everything in the centre of the table – pork mix, lettuce cups, lime wedges, crispy noodles, peanuts, green onion and chilli – and let everyone build their own! To eat, squeeze over lime juice, fold, then munch and crunch.

PREP & COOK TIME
20 mins

SERVES 4

Need dinner on the table in a flash? This warming, creamy, protein-packed dahl is here to save the day. It's bursting with flavour and perfect for mopping up with soft naan bread. No stress, no fuss – just a big bowl of comfort that'll have everyone scraping their bowls clean.

SUPER SPEEDY DIPPY DAHL

WHAT YOU NEED

1 TBSP OLIVE OIL

1 ONION, DICED

1 TBSP CURRY POWDER

1 TBSP CRUSHED GARLIC

1 TBSP CRUSHED GINGER

1 TBSP VEGETABLE STOCK POWDER

1 CUP SPLIT RED LENTILS, RINSED

400G CAN CHICKPEAS, DRAINED

200G CHERRY TOMATOES, HALVED

1 LONG GREEN CHILLI, SLICED (OPTIONAL)

400G CAN COCONUT MILK

JUICE OF 1 LIME

TO SERVE: 1 CUP GREEK YOGHURT, CORIANDER LEAVES AND 4 NAAN BREADS

WHAT YOU DO

Heat the olive oil in a large pan over medium heat. Pop in the onion and cook for 2 minutes or until softened. Now, toss in the curry powder, garlic, ginger and stock powder and stir for 1 minute to toast those spices – it will smell amazing!

Next, add your lentils, chickpeas, cherry tomatoes, chilli, coconut milk and 2 cups water. Bring to the boil, then turn the heat down to low and let it bubble away gently for 15 minutes, giving it a stir now and then to prevent sticking to the base of the pan.

Once it's thick and lovely, turn off the heat and squeeze in the lime juice. Taste and adjust with a little salt to how you like it.

Spoon into bowls, dollop with yoghurt and sprinkle with coriander. Serve with warm naan bread for dunking right in.

PREP & COOK TIME
25 mins

SERVES 4

This weeknight dinner hero is rich, satisfying, and ready in no time. With a few simple ingredients, this stress-free recipe comes together to create a bowl of saucy, sausage and cheesy goodness that makes you look like a legend without breaking a sweat.

GOLDEN SAUSAGE PASTA MAGIC

WHAT YOU NEED

500G PENNE OR RIGATONI

500G FAT PORK SAUSAGES

1 TBSP CRUSHED GARLIC

2 TBSP TOMATO PASTE

1 TBSP CHICKEN STOCK POWDER

1 TBSP DRIED OREGANO

½ TSP GROUND NUTMEG

½ CUP WHITE WINE OR WATER

300ML POURING CREAM

1 CUP GRATED PARMESAN

SALT AND PEPPER

WHAT YOU DO

Cook the pasta in a large pan of boiling salted water following the packet instructions. When it's done, scoop out ½ cup pasta cooking water and set aside before draining the pasta.

While the pasta is cooking, heat a large frying pan over high heat. Remove the skins from the sausages. Add the meat straight into the hot pan (no oil needed). Let it sizzle away, breaking up the sausage meat with a spoon, for 5 minutes or until golden and crispy.

Now, pop in the garlic, tomato paste, chicken stock powder, dried oregano and ground nutmeg. Give it a good stir and cook for 1 minute or until everything gets toasty. Pour in the wine and cream. Turn the heat down to medium and let it bubble away for 5 minutes or until reduced by half.

Sprinkle half the parmesan into the pan. Stir through until melted and the sauce is creamy. Tip in the cooked pasta and splash of the reserved pasta water to make everything glossy and saucy. Give it all a good stir. Taste to see if it needs a pinch of salt and pepper. Then, dish it up in big bowls, and sprinkle with the remaining parmesan for good measure.

PREP & COOK TIME
25 mins

STEPH SAYS

IF YOU'VE NEVER COOKED WITH SAUSAGE MEAT BEFORE, DON'T WORRY, WE'RE JUST DITCHING THE SKINS AND LETTING THE PAN DO THE MAGIC!

SET & FORGET

Let your oven, slow cooker or air fryer do the hard work for you. These hands-off meals are made for busy days, long to-do lists, and anyone who wants to gain back time with dinner that cooks itself.

AIR FRYER PORK POPSTARS

Let's talk about pork belly. Once you've nailed these crispy, sticky little bites of heavenly pork, you can serve them five delicious ways — bao buns, salad, fried rice, stir-fry, or rice bowls — for your dinner wins.

SERVES 4

STICKY PORK BELLY BITES

WHAT YOU NEED

2 TSP SALT

2 TSP GARLIC POWDER

1 TBSP CHINESE FIVE SPICE

1KG PORK BELLY, CUT INTO BITE-SIZED PIECES

FOR THE STICKY SAUCE

2 TBSP DARK SOY SAUCE

2 TBSP HONEY

1 TBSP OYSTER SAUCE

1 TSP CRUSHED GINGER

1 TSP CRUSHED GARLIC

JUICE OF 1 LIME

1 TSP CHILLI POWDER (OPTIONAL)

WHAT YOU DO

Combine the salt, garlic powder and five spice. Then, toss your pork belly pieces with the spice mix.

Arrange your spiced pork belly pieces in your air fryer in one layer. Don't worry if you can't fit them all at once, you can always do a second batch.

Set the temperature to 200°C and the time for 15 minutes, then cook, giving them a shake halfway through to ensure even cooking.

While your pork is sizzling away, get started on the sticky sauce: whisk together the sauce ingredients in a large bowl to combine.

When your pork belly bites are crispy and golden, toss in the sticky sauce, so every piece is sticky and shiny. Return them to the air fryer basket. Set the temperature to 200°C and the time for 5 minutes, then cook until sticky and glazed. Serve straight up or turn into dinner magic!

PREP & COOK TIME
30 mins

STICKY PORK BELLY BAO BUNS

Steam 12 frozen bao buns following the packet instructions.

In a bowl, mix 250g coleslaw mix, ½ bunch coriander leaves, juice of 1 lime, 1 tsp each caster sugar and salt. In another bowl, mix ½ cup mayonnaise and 1 tbsp hot sauce or sweet chilli sauce.

Fill bao with slaw, 500g reheated sticky pork belly bites, the chilli mayo and sliced fresh chilli if you like it hot.

STICKY PORK BELLY NOODLE STIR-FRY

Microwave 400g Hokkien noodles for 1–2 minutes to loosen. Heat a splash of oil in a wok or large frying pan.

Add 2 sliced red capsicums, 1 bunch chopped broccolini, 1 sliced red onion, 2 sliced green onions and 1 tbsp each crushed garlic and crushed ginger. Stir-fry for 4 minutes or until veggies start to soften.

Add the noodles and ¼ cup oyster sauce, 2 tbsp light soy sauce and 1 tbsp sweet chilli sauce. Toss like a boss until it is all coated and glossy. Scoop into bowls and top with 500g hot sticky pork belly bites. Chopsticks are optional but fun!

STICKY PORK BELLY ASIAN SALAD

Toss together 300g pkt coleslaw, 2 diced Lebanese cucumbers, ½ bunch mint leaves, ½ bunch coriander leaves, ½ cup roasted peanuts and 100g pkt crunchy fried noodles.

In a bowl, whisk the juice of 1 lime with 1 tbsp each fish sauce and sweet chilli sauce until combined. Pour the dressing over the salad. Give it a shake to coat.

Pile the salad into it bowls and top with 500g hot pork belly bites. Serve with lime wedges and fresh sliced chilli.

STICKY PORK BELLY RICE BOWLS

Divide 450g reheated microwave rice among four bowls.

Arrange 1 cup grated carrot, 1 diced cucumber, 1 cup corn kernels and hot sticky pork belly bites on top.

Add soft-boiled or poached eggs (optional) if you're feeling fancy and finish with a drizzle of Kewpie (Japanese mayonnaise) and a sprinkle of green onions.

STICKY PORK BELLY FRIED RICE

Heat a splash of oil in a wok or pan, pour in 4 lightly beaten eggs, then scramble them. Remove egg and set aside. Add another splash of oil to the wok. Cook 1 tbsp crushed garlic, 1 tbsp crushed ginger and 2 cups frozen peas, corn and carrots for 3 minutes or until heated through.

Add 3 cups cold cooked rice and toss until hot. Add 2 tbsp soy sauce, 1 tbsp oyster sauce and the scrambled eggs and toss again.

Turn off the heat and mix through 1 bunch sliced coriander leaves. Scoop into bowls, top with 500g pork belly bites and 2 sliced green onions. Dig in!

CHICKEN PARCEL PARTY PACKS

SERVES 4

This weeknight wonder of juicy chicken, buttery potatoes, green beans and zingy lemon are all wrapped up in their own little parcels, so there are no pans to wash. It's like a flavour present that cooks itself! All you do is pop them in the oven or air fryer and dinner is DONE.

WHAT YOU NEED

2 MEDIUM POTATOES

400G GREEN BEANS

1 LEMON

4 CHICKEN BREASTS

2 TSP GROUND CUMIN

SALT AND PEPPER

80G BUTTER

TO SERVE: PARSLEY

WHAT YOU DO

Slice your potatoes slightly thinner than a 5-cent coin! Trim your beans so they're all neat and tidy. Trim the ends off your lemon and discard them, then slice the rest into 8 thin rounds. Sprinkle the chicken breasts on both sides with cumin, salt and pepper.

Tear off 4 long sheets of foil – large enough to wrap your dinner up like a big silver pillow. Pop a sheet of baking paper on top of each piece of foil – this will stop food sticking and keeps it fancy.

Lay the potato slices, slightly overlapping, right down the middle to make a bed the same size as the chicken and season with salt and pepper. Then, add a pile of green beans and lay 2 slices of lemon over the beans. Now, perch your chicken breast right on top of the lemon.

Next, pop a big blob of butter on each chicken breast. To wrap your parcels, bring the two long sides of foil up to meet in the middle and fold over a couple of times to seal. Next, fold in the short sides to make a snug parcel.

Pop your parcels into the air fryer basket and set the temperature to 200°C and the timer for 20 minutes or cook in the oven at 220°C for 35 minutes. Carefully open one up (watch out for the hot steam!) and pierce the chicken with a knife or skewer – if the juices run clear and the potatoes are soft, you're good to go. If not, reseal the parcels and return to the air fryer for a further 5 minutes or oven for 10 minutes. Serve with parsley.

PREP & COOK TIME
35 mins

SERVES 4

Crispy on the outside, fluffy on the inside, these jacket potatoes are the ultimate lazy dinner hero. They're speedy, cheap, and a blank canvas to top with any leftovers. Think chilli con carne, Bolognese, curry or chicken mornay with a dollop of something creamy.

CRISPY POTATO DINNER BOMBS

WHAT YOU NEED

4 LARGE POTATOES (ABOUT 280G EACH)

COOKING OIL SPRAY

2 TBSP BUTTER

SALT AND PEPPER

WHAT YOU DO

Wash your potatoes and prick them all over with a fork about 6 times each – this will stop them exploding in the microwave which, trust me, you don't want!

Pop them in the microwave and cook on HIGH for 7–10 minutes or until cooked through. They should feel soft when you squeeze them, but not mushy.

Transfer the cooked potatoes to your air fryer basket and spray generously with oil – this will make them crispy. Set the temperature to 200°C and the timer for 8 minutes, cook until crispy on the outside.

Take them out and carefully cut a deep cross into each potato. Hold the potato with a clean tea towel and give it a little squeeze to reveal the white centre. Add 2 teaspoons butter and fluff with a fork, then season with salt and pepper.

Now, the fun part. Load them up with whatever reheated leftover you have on hand: stew, curry, meatballs, or my Boss-Level Bolognese (page 76), Big-Batch Tex-Mex Chilli (page 79) or Creamy Chicken Mornay Magic (page 80). Top with cheese, sour cream, yoghurt, or just gobble them as they are.

PREP & COOK TIME
25 mins

SERVES 4

This one's a total weeknight winner. Easy, comforting and packed with flavour, these dumplings are the perfect answer for when you want something delish without the drama. Just throw it all in a baking dish and let the oven work its magic.

COSY CURRY SAUCE DUMPLINGS

WHAT YOU NEED

1 TSP CRUSHED GARLIC

1 TSP CRUSHED GINGER

1 TBSP BROWN SUGAR

2 TBSP THAI RED CURRY PASTE

¼ CUP LIGHT SOY SAUCE

JUICE OF 1 LIME

400ML CAN COCONUT MILK

20 FROZEN DUMPLINGS (NOT SOUP DUMPLINGS)

3 BULBS BOK CHOY, QUARTERED LENGTHWAYS

TO SERVE: SLICED GREEN ONIONS, CORIANDER LEAVES AND CRUNCHY CHILLI OIL

WHAT YOU DO

Preheat your oven to 200°C.

Grab a large ovenproof dish and pop in the garlic, ginger, brown sugar, red curry paste, soy sauce, lime juice and coconut milk. Give it a good whisk until it looks smooth and smells amazing.

Scatter the frozen dumplings over the sauce and give them a little nudge to coat in the saucy goodness. Now, snuggle the chopped bok choy on top of the dumplings, spreading it out so it all gets a bit of sauce-love.

Cover the dish tightly with foil or a lid so none of the steamy goodness escapes. Pop into the oven and cook for 25 minutes. Go put your feet up!

Once it's done, remove the foil and top with sliced green onions, coriander leaves or a spoonful of chilli oil if you like things spicy.

PREP & COOK TIME
35 mins

MOROCCAN CHICKEN MAGIC TRAY BAKE

SERVES 4

This one-tray wonder is bursting with sunny Mediterranean flavours and takes hardly any effort at all. Juicy chicken, sweet roast veggies and golden chickpeas all soak up the most fabulous Moroccan marinade while the oven does the work. Add a garlicky yoghurt drizzle and you've got yourself a no-fuss dinner party on a tray!

WHAT YOU NEED

- 2 TBSP MOROCCAN SPICE MIX
- 1 TBSP CRUSHED GARLIC
- 2 TSP SALT
- ¼ CUP OLIVE OIL
- JUICE OF 1 LEMON
- 2 RED ONIONS
- 2 RED CAPSICUMS
- 250G CHERRY TOMATOES
- 400G CAN CHICKPEAS, DRAINED
- 6–8 CHICKEN THIGH FILLETS
- TO SERVE: SPRIGS OF CORIANDER

FOR THE CORIANDER YOGHURT SAUCE

- 1 CUP GREEK YOGHURT
- ½ BUNCH CORIANDER, CHOPPED
- JUICE OF ½ LEMON
- 1 TSP SALT

WHAT YOU DO

Preheat your oven to 200°C.

Let's start with the magic flavour bomb. In a large bowl, whisk together the Moroccan spice mix, garlic, salt, olive oil and lemon juice. Cut each onion into 8 chunky wedges. Then, slice your capsicums into pieces roughly the same size as the onion.

Line a large baking tray with baking paper – less mess and more yay!

Pop your onion, capsicum, tomatoes, chickpeas and chicken onto your prepared tray. Pour over your flavour bomb. Use your hands to mix everything until well combined and glistening, making sure to spread it out evenly. Pop it in the oven for 30 minutes or until golden and smelling amazing.

While it's baking, make the coriander yoghurt sauce: stir all the ingredients together to make a creamy delicious drizzle.

Serve everything straight from the tray with a dollop of the yoghurt sauce on the side and sprigs of coriander on top.

PREP & COOK TIME
45 mins

STEPH SAYS

IF YOU'RE USING AN AIR FRYER, DOUBLE-CHECK YOUR DISH FITS.

SERVES 4

This one's for the days when you want something fancy without the faff. Crispy-skin salmon meets buttery broccolini and roasted lemons that turn zingy and golden in the oven – it's the kind of dinner wizardry that tastes like it took way more effort than it did.

ONE-TRAY MISO SALMON MIRACLE

WHAT YOU NEED

2 BUNCHES BROCCOLINI

2 LEMONS

COOKING OIL SPRAY

1 TBSP WHITE MISO PASTE

1 TBSP HONEY

1 TBSP OLIVE OIL

4 SKIN-ON SALMON FILLETS

SALT

WHAT YOU DO

Preheat your oven to 200°C or air fryer to 180°C.

First, line your baking tray with baking paper, so there's no sticking or scrubbing! Lay your broccolini across the tray in one big green tangle. Then, sprinkle with a good pinch of salt and cheeky spray of oil. Cut the lemons in half and pop face-up at the tray edges.

In a little bowl, mix the miso, honey and olive oil – this is your sticky, salty flavour bomb.

Place the salmon fillets skin-side down on top of the broccolini. Brush the tops and sides of each fillet with your flavour bomb mix, until glossy. Now, flip the salmon skin-side facing up. And spray the skin with a little oil and sprinkle with salt – this will help crisp the skin. Pop the tray in your oven for 15 minutes or air fryer for 10 minutes.

When the salmon is done and the lemons are looking toasty, flip the salmon skin-side down, squeeze the roasted lemon halves over the top and dig in.

PREP & COOK TIME
25 mins

SERVES 4

This Chinese-style roast chicken is full of big flavours. We're talking juicy chook and grapes bursting with sticky goodness roasted on a bed of cabbage that soaks up all the flavour. It's one tray: made for a dramatic reveal, with no fuss. It's perfect for when you want something bold and beautiful without the need for a culinary degree.

ROAST CHICKEN MEETS CHINATOWN

WHAT YOU NEED

2KG WHOLE CHICKEN

1 SMALL RED CABBAGE

2 CUPS RED GRAPES

¼ CUP HOISIN SAUCE

2 TSP CHINESE FIVE SPICE

1 TBSP CRUSHED GARLIC

1 TBSP CRUSHED GINGER

2 TSP SALT

TO SERVE: SLICED GREEN ONION

WHAT YOU DO

Preheat your oven to 200°C.

Grab your kitchen scissors or a sharp knife and cut down either side of the chicken's backbone and discard the bone. Flip the chicken skin-side up and press down on the breast to flatten it out.

Cut the red cabbage into 2cm-thick rounds, as wide as 2 fingers. Line a tray with baking paper and lay out your cabbage slices in a single layer. Scatter the grapes over the cabbage and sprinkle with a little salt and pepper. Lay your chicken flat on top of the cabbage and grapes.

In a small bowl, whisk together the hoisin, five spice, garlic, ginger and salt until combined and it smells fab.

Pour your flavour bomb all over the chicken and give it a good massage so every bit is covered in sauce. Pop it into the oven and roast for 60 minutes.

To check if it's ready, stab a knife into the thickest part of the thigh. If the juice runs clear, you're good to go! If not, place it back in the oven for a further 10 minutes. Once cooked, cut the chicken into quarters and serve with the roasted cabbage, grapes and sliced green onion.

PREP & COOK TIME
1¼ hrs

STEPH SAYS

DON'T FORGET TO SERVE YOUR CHICKEN WITH ALL THOSE STICKY, TASTY PAN JUICES.

SERVES 4

These sticky, sweet pork chops with apple are a total show-off meal that feels fancy but couldn't be easier. Everything cooks together in the air fryer for the kind of dinner that makes your kitchen smell amazing and gets gobbled up in no time. Grab your chops and let's get cracking!

SIZZLE UP PORK & APPLE

WHAT YOU NEED

4 PORK CUTLETS

300G GREEN BEANS

2 GREEN APPLES

1 TBSP CRUSHED GARLIC

1 TBSP HONEY

1 TBSP DIJON MUSTARD

1 TBSP SMOKED PAPRIKA

¼ CUP OLIVE OIL

SALT AND PEPPER

WHAT YOU DO

Snip the fatty edge of your pork chops using scissors or a knife – about 6 little cuts around the edge. This little trick will help keep them nice and flat while they cook. Sprinkle the chops with a little salt and pepper.

Next, trim the ends off your beans and cut your apples into quarters. Cut out the core, then cut each quarter in half again so you end up with 16 chunky wedges.

In a large bowl, whisk together the garlic, honey, Dijon mustard, paprika and olive oil. Then, toss the pork chops in the sauce until coated and glossy.

Pop your beans and apple wedges into the air fryer basket and sprinkle with salt. Lay the pork chops on top of the beans and apples, snug as a bug. Set the temperature to 200°C and the timer for 15–20 minutes and cook, flipping the chops and giving the beans and apples a little shake halfway through.

Once they're done (don't skip this bit), pour the delicious juice from the bottom of your air fryer all over the top when you serve. It's liquid gold!

PREP & COOK TIME
30 mins

SERVES 4

Lamb chops in the oven? Yes please! This one-tray flavour wonder is yet another midweek hero. Tender, juicy lamb chops roasted alongside sweet, caramelised veggies, all jazzed up with a zippy little flavour bomb. And all you need to do is pop it on a tray, whack it in the oven, and get ready for the dinner yum!

SLAMMIN' LAMB TRAY BAKE

WHAT YOU NEED

2 MEDIUM SWEET POTATOES (ABOUT 350G EACH)

1 SMALL CAULIFLOWER

4 LAMB FOREQUARTER CHOPS

2 TSP GROUND CUMIN

2 TSP LEMON PEPPER

2 TBSP RED WINE VINEGAR

2 TSP SALT

¼ CUP OLIVE OIL

TO SERVE: CORIANDER OR PARSLEY LEAVES, AND LEMON WEDGES

WHAT YOU DO

Preheat your oven to 200°C.

While that's happening, peel your sweet potatoes. Then, chop them in half lengthways and cut into chunky 4cm pieces. Next, cut up the cauliflower into 4cm pieces to match.

Line a large baking tray with baking paper – because no one likes scrubbing trays. Then, pop your lamb chops and veggies onto the prepared tray.

In a little bowl, mix the cumin, lemon pepper, red wine vinegar, salt and olive oil. This is your lamb flavour bomb. Pour over the tray then get your hands in there to coat the lamb and veggies nice and evenly, spreading them out so nothing is sitting on top of each other.

Bake for 30 minutes or until the lamb is cooked through. Then, serve with a sprinkle of herbs and a cheeky lemon wedge if you're feeling fancy.

PREP & COOK TIME
45 mins

STEPH SAYS

KEEP THE VEGGIES SIZES SIMILAR, SO EVERYTHING COOKS EVENLY.

SLOW COOKER DUMP BAG DREAM DINNERS

Want dinners that pretty much cook themselves, without the stress or mess? These freeze-ahead slow cooker dump bag recipes are your lifesavers for busy weeks, unexpected guests or when you just can't be bothered. Prep the recipe, pack it into a zip-lock bag, freeze and thaw, then dump it into the slow cooker and let it do its thing. Bingo!

SERVES 4

CHICKEN TIKKA MASALA

Pop 1kg halved chicken thighs, 2 tsp salt, 2 sliced red onions, 1 tbsp each crushed garlic, crushed ginger, sugar and garam masala, 400g crushed tomatoes, 2 tbsp balsamic vinegar and ½ cup tikka masala paste into a zip-lock bag. Seal the bag and massage the contents to mix everything together.

Open the bag slightly, squeeze out the air, reseal and flatten. Label and date, then freeze for up to 1 month to cook later.

To cook, thaw in the fridge overnight. Tip the contents of the bag into a 5.5L (22-cup) slow cooker. Pop the lid on your slow cooker and set it to LOW for 8 hours or HIGH for 4 hours.

To finish, stir through ½ cup pouring cream. Then, taste the sauce and adjust the flavour with a little more salt, sugar or vinegar if it needs it. Sprinkle with coriander leaves and serve over rice with a dollop of Greek yoghurt.

SERVES 4, WITH LEFTOVERS

MOROCCAN BEEF & CHICKPEAS

Pop 1kg diced chuck steak, 2 tbsp Moroccan spice mix, 1 tbsp crushed garlic, 1 diced onion, 2 sliced carrots, 1 tbsp beef stock powder, 6 dried pitted dates and 400g can drained chickpeas into a zip-lock bag. Seal the bag and massage the contents to mix everything together.

Zip, squish, flatten, label and freeze for up to 1 month to cook later. Defrost overnight in the fridge, then dump into your slow cooker. Cook on LOW for 8 hours or HIGH for 4 hours. To finish, if you want it thicker, combine 1 tbsp cornflour and ¼ cup water, pour it in and cook on HIGH for a further 15 minutes.

Serve with rice or couscous, a large spoonful of Greek yoghurt and sprigs of parsley if you like.

SERVES 4

SPANISH-STYLE CHICKEN

Pop 4 chicken thigh cutlets (bone-in), 2 cured sliced chorizo, 1 sliced red onion, 2 diced red capsicums, 1 tbsp crushed garlic, 2 tbsp smoked paprika, 1 tbsp ground cumin, 400g can crushed tomatoes and a 450g jar of drained stuffed Spanish olives in a large zip-lock bag.

Zip, squish, flatten, label and freeze for up to 1 month to cook later. Defrost overnight in the fridge, then dump into your slow cooker. Cook on LOW for 8 hours or HIGH for 4 hours.

Stir in 1 bunch chopped parsley. Serve with lemon wedges, extra parsley and buttery baby potatoes, mash or rice. Yum!

SERVES 4

LAMB RAGU

Dice 1 each: carrot, onion and celery stalk. Pop into a large zip-lock bag with 4 lamb shanks, 700g jar tomato passata, 2 tsp each dried rosemary and thyme and 1 tbsp chicken stock powder.

Zip, squish, flatten, label and freeze for up to one month to cook later. Defrost overnight in the fridge, then dump into your slow cooker. Cook on LOW for 8 hours or HIGH for 4 hours.

Once it's cooked, pull the meat off the bones, shred it and stir it back into the sauce. Taste it to see if it needs salt and pepper, then stir through 1 bunch chopped parsley and zest of 1 lemon. Serve over Freezer Stash Mash (page 83) or whatever you've got!

SERVES 4, WITH LEFTOVERS

BEEF STROGANOFF

Pop 1kg diced beef chuck steak, 2 diced onions, 400g halved mushrooms, ¼ cup tomato paste, 2 tbsp Worcestershire sauce, 2 tbsp paprika and 1 tbsp crushed garlic into a large zip-lock bag. Zip, squish, flatten, label and freeze for up to 1 month to cook later.

Defrost overnight in the fridge, then dump into your slow cooker. Cook on LOW for 8 hours or HIGH for 4 hours. Mix 1 tbsp cornflour with ¼ cup water and stir it into the cooker.

Cook, uncovered on HIGH for 15 minutes to thicken. Stir through ½ cup sour cream and ½ cup chopped parsley. Serve with mash or pasta and dive in.

COOK ONCE, FEAST TWICE

—

This chapter is your new best friend for busy nights and budget wins! These recipes are all about big-batch brilliance, where one round of cooking gives you a delicious dinner now and a head start on another meal later.

PERFECTLY ROASTED CHICKEN

SERVES 4

Sometimes the best dinners are the ones you've already half-made! These delicious chicken recipes are perfect for freezing and pulling out when dinner feels just too hard. Pick a marinade style, match it to your choice of chicken, then choose how you want to cook – oven, air-fry, pan-fry or barbecue. Future you will be giving you a big ol' high five!

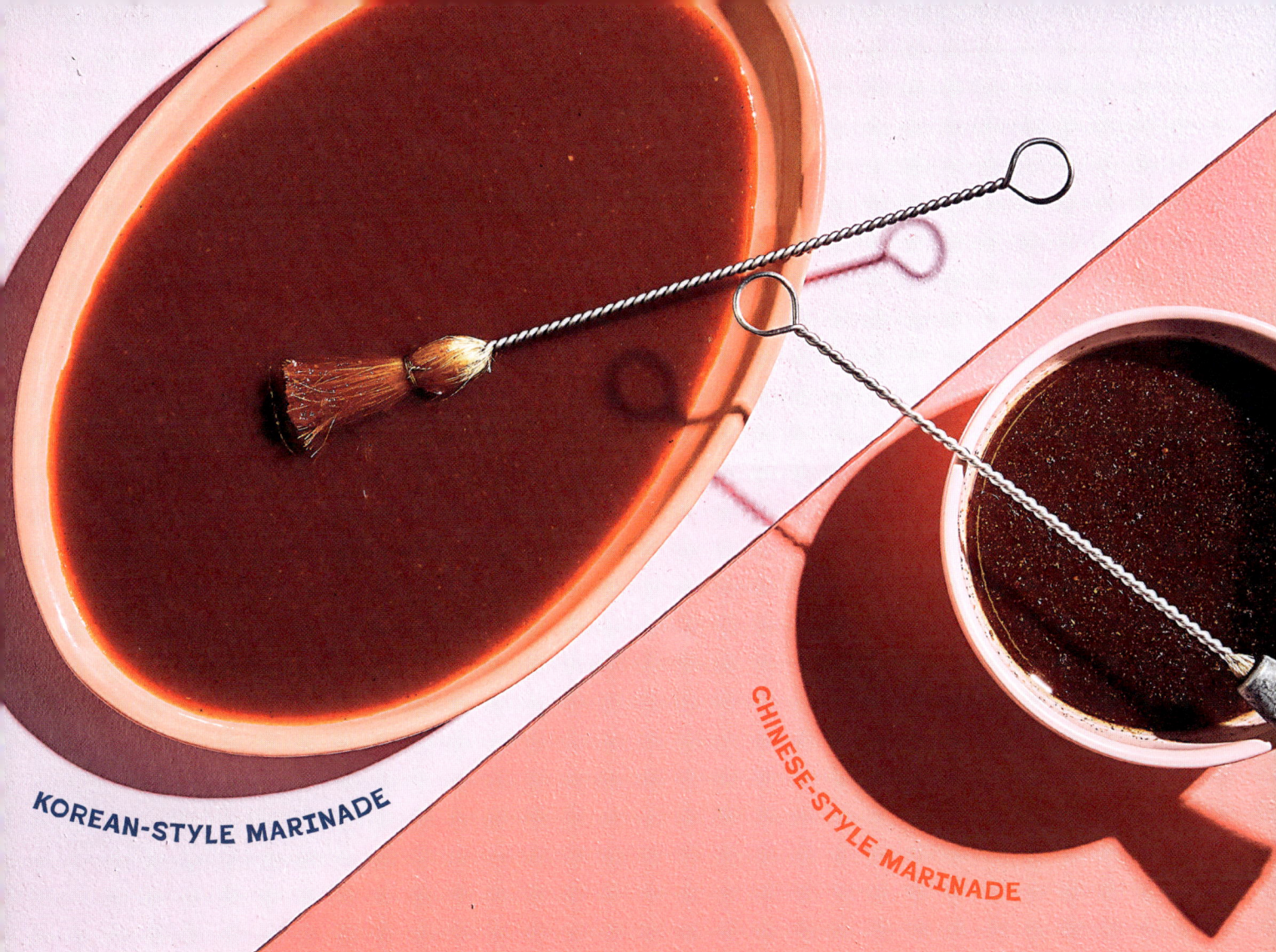

KOREAN-STYLE MARINADE

CHINESE-STYLE MARINADE

1. PICK A MARINADE

KOREAN-STYLE

2 tbsp gochujang, 1 tbsp each brown sugar, crushed garlic, light soy sauce, apple cider vinegar and neutral oil.

CHINESE-STYLE

1 tbsp each soy sauce, oyster sauce, honey, crushed ginger, Chinese cooking wine, neutral oil and 1 tsp Chinese five spice.

INDIAN-STYLE

1 cup Greek yoghurt, 1 tbsp each crushed garlic, crushed ginger, garam masala and 2 tsp chilli powder (optional), 2 tsp salt and Juice of 1 lime.

MOROCCAN-STYLE

1 cup Greek yoghurt, 1 tbsp Moroccan spice mix, 2 tsp salt, 1 tsp crushed ginger, 1 tsp crushed garlic, Juice of ½ lemon.

STEPH'S SPICY FAVE

½ cup each mayonnaise and Greek yoghurt, 1 bunch coriander (including stems), 8 sliced pickled jalapeños, 2 tbsp pickled jalapeños juice, 1 tbsp crushed garlic, 2 tsp salt, 1 tsp smoked paprika and 1 tsp ground cumin.

2. PICK YOUR CHICKEN

ANY CUT WORKS!

Use 4 breasts or thigh cutlets, or 8 thigh fillets, or 2kg wings or drumsticks, or a whole butterflied chicken.

WHAT YOU DO

For all marinades, except Steph's Spicy Fave, pop the ingredients in a large zip-lock bag. Give the bag a squish to mix, then add your chicken of choice and massage to coat.

Next, squeeze out the air, seal the bag, and flatten it out.

For Steph's Spicy Fave, whizz everything in a blender until smooth and green. Then, pour into a large zip-lock bag with chicken of choice and massage to coat.

Now either pop in the fridge to marinate for a few hours or overnight, or freeze for a rainy-day dinner save (before cooking, thaw in the fridge overnight).

STEPH'S SPICY FAVE

INDIAN-STYLE MARINADE

MOROCCAN-STYLE MARINADE

3. PICK A COOKING STYLE

AIR FRYER

Bone-in chicken
200°C for 20–30 mins

Boneless chicken
200°C for 10–15 mins

Butterflied (split) chicken
200°C for 40–50 mins

OVEN

Bone-in chicken
200°C for 30–40 mins

Boneless chicken
200°C for 20–25 mins

Butterflied (split) chicken
200°C for 50–60 mins

PAN-FRIED OR BARBECUED

Bone-in chicken
Medium-high heat for 25–30 mins

Boneless chicken
Medium-high heat for 15–20 mins

Butterflied (split) chicken
Cook skin-side down for 15 mins, then flip and finish in the oven or BBQ with the lid down for 45–50 mins

STEPH SAYS

REST IS BEST. TAKE YOUR CHICKEN OUT OF THE FRIDGE 30 MINUTES BEFORE COOKING. AFTER COOKING, COVER LOOSELY IN FOIL AND REST FOR 10 MINUTES TO KEEP THE JUICES INSIDE.

4. CHECK IT'S READY

Stick a skewer or sharp knife into the thickest part of the chicken. If the juices run clear, you're good to go. Still pink? Give it a few more minutes. Got a meat thermometer? You're aiming for 75°C inside.

BACHELOR'S HANDBAG DINNER HACKS

Let's talk about the ultimate dinner hack – a good ol' roast chook! Buy a whole roast chicken, or make your own by cooking a Perfectly Roasted Chicken (page 66), using your favourite marinade and cooking style for a whole butterflied (split) chicken. Perfect for when you're short on time but still want something that tastes like a treat.

MAKES 12

CHICKEN & CHEESE CHIMICHANGAS

Shred the meat from half a roast chicken, discarding the skin and bones. In a large bowl, mix the shredded chicken, 1 cup grated cheddar, 200g Mexican tomato salsa, 1 diced red capsicum, 400g can drained black beans and 1 bunch chopped coriander. Lay out 12 small (16cm) tortillas and divide the mix between them. Fold in the sides, then roll up like little burrito parcels, so nothing escapes. Pop folded side down in the air fryer and spray with oil. Set the temperature to 200°C and the timer for 8 minutes. Cook, flipping and spraying again halfway through cooking. Serve with sour cream, shredded lettuce and extra salsa.

Tip: Arrange them in a small foil tray and spray with oil.

PREP & COOK TIME
20 mins

SERVES 4

QUICK CHICKEN NOODLE SOUP

Shred the meat from half a roast chicken, discarding the skin and bones. Dice 1 onion, 1 carrot, 1 celery stalk and 2 potatoes. Heat a drizzle of oil in a large pan over medium heat. Cook diced veggies with 1 tbsp crushed garlic for 5 minutes.

Add ½ bunch chopped parsley, the shredded chicken and 2L chicken stock. Bring to a boil, then simmer, covered, for 15 minutes. Squeeze in the juice of 1 lemon and season to taste. While that's happening, cook 4 x 85g pkts 2-minute noodles without the flavour sachets, drain and divide among bowls.

Ladle the soup over the noodles and top with parsley. Serve with a spoonful of chilli oil if you like it spicy!

PREP & COOK TIME
30 mins

SERVES 2

THE BEST CHICKEN SALAD OR SANDWICH

Shred or dice the meat from half a roast chicken, discarding the skin and bones. In a large bowl, whisk ¼ cup each Greek yoghurt and mayonnaise, 1 tsp Dijon mustard, juice of ½ lemon and ½ tsp each salt and cracked pepper.

Dice 2 celery stalks, 1 small red onion and 6–8 dill pickles. Then, add to the dressing with ½ cup halved seedless red grapes, ½ cup roasted walnuts, ¼ cup finely chopped dill and the chicken, and mix to coat. Serve in lettuce cups, wraps or between slices of bread for a sandwich that slaps.

PREP TIME
15 mins

SERVES 4

EASY CHICKEN & MUSHROOM RISOTTO

Shred or dice the meat from half a roast chicken, discarding the skin and bones. Heat a drizzle of oil in a large pan over medium heat, cook 1 diced onion, 100g diced bacon and 250g sliced mushrooms until golden and smelling amazing.

Stir in 1½ cups arborio rice and cook for 2 minutes. Add ½ cup wine, cook until reduced by half. Then, add 1.5L chicken stock, cook, stirring every now and then, for 20 minutes (adding the chicken during the last 5 minutes), or until the rice is just tender and the stock is absorbed.

Add a splash more water if needed. Stir in 50g each butter and grated parmesan, juice of ½ lemon and ½ cup chopped parsley. Serve topped with extra parmesan.

PREP & COOK TIME
30 mins

SERVES 4

CHEAT'S CHICKEN BIRYANI

Shred or dice the meat from half a roast chicken, discarding the skin and bones. Heat a drizzle of oil in a large pan over medium heat. Add 1 diced onion, 1 diced red capsicum and 1 tbsp crushed garlic, cook for 2 minutes. Stir in 1 tsp chilli flakes, 3 tsp curry powder and 2 tsp garam masala and cook for 1 minute.

Add the chicken and 1½ cups basmati rice and stir to coat in spices. Stir in 1½ cups chicken stock, followed by 400ml can coconut milk and bring to a boil. Turn the heat to low, pop the lid on and cook for 15 minutes or until the rice has absorbed the liquid.

Turn off the heat. Quickly lift the lid and scatter over 100g frozen peas. Replace the lid and stand for 10 minutes to heat peas. Serve scattered with ¼ cup chopped coriander and lime wedges.

PREP & COOK TIME
35 mins

SERVES 8, WITH LEFTOVERS

This one's a freezer-friendly superstar and a total veggie smuggler! It makes a big ol' batch perfect for pasta nights, jaffles, baked potatoes, lasagne layers or a next-level pasta bake. I like to blitz the veggies in the food processor so the kids can't spot them, but you do you, Boo!

BOSS-LEVEL BOLOGNESE

WHAT YOU NEED

- 6 CARROTS
- 1 SMALL BUNCH CELERY
- 4 ONIONS
- ½ CUP OLIVE OIL
- 1KG PORK AND BEEF MINCE
- ½ CUP TOMATO PASTE
- 250G FROZEN SPINACH
- ⅓ CUP CHICKEN STOCK POWDER
- 2 TSP DRIED THYME
- 2 TSP DRIED ROSEMARY
- 2 TSP DRIED OREGANO
- 2 TSP CASTER SUGAR OR 1 CUP RED WINE
- 2 X 700G JARS TOMATO PASSATA

WHAT YOU DO

Grab your food processor (or your knife and chopping board if you're feeling old-school) and blitz your carrots, celery and onions in batches until finely chopped.

Heat up the olive oil in a large heavy-based pan over medium heat. Toss in your veggie mix and your mince. Now break up that mince like your life depends on it – no big lumps allowed! Once the meat has browned, stir in the tomato paste.

Now, add everything else – spinach, chicken stock powder herbs, sugar or wine, passata and ½ jar of water (use the tomato passata jar to measure). Give it all a good stir. Bring it up to a bubbly boil, then drop the heat to low and gently simmer for an hour or two. Give it a stir every now and then and add a splash of water if it starts looking too thick.

No time to babysit the stove? Pop it in a 5.5L (22-cup) slow cooker without the water, pop on the lid and cook on HIGH for 4 hours or LOW for 8 hours.

Allow to cool, then divide the sauce between two large zip-lock bags. Lie the bags flat and squeeze out the air and seal. Label and date, then freeze lying flat for up to 3 months.

To use, thaw overnight in the fridge. Stir through cooked pasta, or serve over baked potatoes, in a jaffle, or as a lasagne or other baked pasta filling. Yum!

PREP & COOK TIME
2 hrs

SERVES 8

BIG-BATCH TEX-MEX CHILLI

This hearty American-style chilli is meaty, rich, and packed with flavour, perfect for batch cooking and turning into all kinds of easy dinners, from nachos to tacos and burritos and more!

WHAT YOU NEED

- OLIVE OIL, TO DRIZZLE
- 1KG BEEF MINCE
- 2 TBSP CRUSHED GARLIC
- 2 ONIONS, DICED
- 2 RED CAPSICUMS, DICED
- ½ CUP TOMATO PASTE
- ⅓ CUP BEEF STOCK POWDER
- 2 X 40G PKTS TACO SEASONING MIX (OR MAKE YOUR OWN, PAGE 84)
- 2 TSP CHILLI POWDER (OPTIONAL)
- 2 TSP CASTER SUGAR
- 2 X 800G CANS CRUSHED TOMATOES
- 3 X 400G CANS KIDNEY BEANS, DRAINED

WHAT YOU DO

Heat a drizzle of oil in a large pan over medium heat. Toss in mince and break it up with a wooden spoon. Now don't touch it! Let it sizzle until brown underneath. Once browned, give it another stir, then throw in your garlic, onions and capsicum. Stir for 5 minutes or until onions are starting to soften.

Now, add everything else, including chilli powder (if you like it spicy) and 1 cup water. Stir and bring to the boil. Turn the heat down to low-medium and cook for 30 minutes or until thickened.

Cool, then divide between two large zip-lock bags. Lie the bags flat, squeeze out the air and seal. Label and date, then freeze lying flat for up to 3 months. Before reheating, thaw overnight in the fridge.

PREP & COOK TIME
1 hr

5 WAYS TO MAKE IT A MEAL

CRISPY NACHOS
Mix grated Mexican cheese with warm corn chips until melted. Top with 1 bag Tex-Mex Chilli, sour cream, guac and diced tomatoes and onion.

TACOS, BURRITOS OR BOWLS
Reheat 1 bag Tex-Mex Chilli to fill taco shells, burritos or a bowl with rice and fresh toppings.

CHILLI RISONI
Bring to the boil 1 bag Tex-Mex Chilli with 1 cup water. Add 1 cup risoni. Reduce heat and cook for 8–10 minutes until tender. Top with sour cream.

JACKET POTATO MAGIC
Make Crispy Potato Dinner Bombs (see page 44) and top with 1 bag reheated Tex-Mex Chilli and cheese.

TACO LASAGNE
In a baking dish, stack 8 tortillas, 1 bag Tex-Mex Chilli and 3 cups grated cheddar in three layers finishing with cheese. Bake at 180°C for 30 minutes or until golden and bubbling.

SERVES 4

Creamy, cheesy, and loaded with goodies – this mornay is a lifesaver because you can make one big batch, then turn it into TWO dinners with barely any extra work. It freezes like a dream and can become a pasta bake, potato topper, pie filling and more. Let's get cooking!

CREAMY CHICKEN MORNAY MAGIC

WHAT YOU NEED

- 1 HEAD BROCCOLI, CUT INTO FLORETS
- OLIVE OIL, TO DRIZZLE
- WHOLE PERFECT ROAST CHICKEN (PAGE 66), SKIN AND BONES DISCARDED, MEAT SHREDDED
- 200G DICED BACON
- 300G MUSHROOMS, SLICED
- 125G BUTTER
- ⅓ CUP PLAIN FLOUR
- 2 TBSP CHICKEN STOCK POWDER
- 3 CUPS MILK
- 1 CUP GRATED PARMESAN CHEESE
- SALT AND PEPPER

WHAT YOU DO

Bring a pan of salted water to the boil and cook broccoli for a quick 3 minutes. Drain and set aside.

Drizzle a large pan with oil and heat over medium heat. Then, throw in your bacon and mushrooms. Cook for 5 minutes or until they smell amazing and start to go golden. Pour in ¼ cup of water and scrape the base of the pan with a wooden spoon to release all the yummy browned bits.

Add your butter and let it melt, then sprinkle over the flour and chicken stock powder. Stir until you can't see any flour. Slowly pour in the milk, whisking as you go. Continue whisking until the sauce starts to bubble and thicken like magic. Turn off the heat, then stir in your parmesan, broccoli and shredded chicken. Give it a taste and season with a little salt and let it cool, then divide it into two large zip-lock bags if you want to freeze it.

Flatten then seal, label, date and freeze for another night when you need dinner done in a flash. To use, thaw a bag in the fridge overnight.

You can serve this simply over fluffy steamed rice; stirred into cooked penne pasta sprinkled with cheese and baked in the oven; topped with cubed garlic bread and baked in the oven (both at 180°C for 20 minutes); spooned over cheese-topped jacket potatoes and air-fried for a few minutes; or in a pie dish topped with a sheet of puff pastry and baked in the oven at 200°C for 25 minutes until puffed and golden.

PREP & COOK TIME
25 mins

SERVES 4

There's nothing better than having creamy, dreamy mash ready to go in your freezer. This make-ahead beauty is your secret sidekick for quick dinners, saucy mains or sausage nights. Just thaw, reheat and enjoy!

FREEZER STASH MASH

WHAT YOU NEED

2KG ALL-PURPOSE WASHED POTATOES

2 TBSP CHICKEN STOCK POWDER

125G BUTTER, DICED

1 CUP HOT MILK

1 TSP SALT, PLUS EXTRA TO TASTE

WHAT YOU DO

If you're using a hand masher, peel your spuds. If you've got a potato ricer, there's no need to peel, just give them a good rinse. Pop your potatoes whole into a large pan with the stock powder and enough cold water to cover the potatoes plus a hand's width. Turn the heat up high and bring to the boil, then turn down to low-medium until gently bubbling and cook for 20–30 minutes or until a sharp knife slides in easily.

Drain the potatoes and get ready to mash while steamy and hot! Mash with a potato masher or push through your ricer into a large bowl. Toss in the butter, hot milk and salt.

Now, grab a spatula or wooden spoon and gently stir, fold, and swirl until the butter melts and everything turns into creamy mash heaven. Taste and add a little more salt if you reckon it needs it.

Divide your mash into 4 containers – aiming for about 500g in each. Then, label and date. The mash will happily freeze for up to 1 month. To use, thaw a container in the fridge overnight.

To reheat, microwave with a cover until hot. If it's a bit thick, loosen with a splash of milk or a little extra butter.

PREP & COOK TIME
40 mins

SWEET & STICKY MARINADE

Mix ¼ cup soy sauce, 2 tbsp brown sugar or honey, 1 tbsp vinegar or lime juice, and 1 tsp crushed garlic. Use to marinate chicken, pork, tofu or mushrooms. Bake, air-fry or pan-fry until caramelised.

NO-STRESS TACO SEASONING

Mix 1 tbsp smoked paprika, 1 tsp each onion powder, garlic powder, dried oregano and salt with ½ tsp chilli powder (optional). Use 2 tablespoons per 500g mince for instant taco filling.

BUDGET BUTTER CHOOK SPICE MIX

Mix 2 tsp garam masala, 1 tsp each ground turmeric, ground coriander, ground cumin and sweet paprika. Add to a base of sautéed onion, garlic and ginger, with some tomato paste and cream, for an easy butter chicken sauce.

STEPH'S SPRINKLE

Mix 1 tbsp each salt and garlic powder, 2 tsp onion powder, 1 tsp each smoked paprika and dried thyme. Keep in a jar and sprinkle on chicken, potatoes, veggies or anything that needs a bit of jazzing up.

10 FLAVOUR BOMB BASICS & TIPS

STEPH'S LAZY-GIRL GREEK BLEND

Mix zest of 1 lemon with 1 tbsp dried oregano, 1 tsp each garlic powder, onion powder and salt. Sprinkle on lamb chops, roast veggies or potato wedges.

THE BEST BASIC CURRY PASTE

In a blender, blitz 1 onion, 1 tbsp each crushed garlic, curry powder and tomato paste with ¼ cup oil. Store in the fridge and use by the spoonful for quick curries.

HOW TO BALANCE FLAVOUR

Too salty? Add a squeeze of lemon juice. Too spicy? Stir in a little yoghurt or cream or add a pinch of sugar. Too bland? Add a pinch of salt or a splash of vinegar. Taste and tweak cos your tastebuds are the boss!

EASY ASIAN DRESSING

Mix grated garlic clove, 2 tbsp soy sauce, 1 tbsp rice vinegar or lemon juice, 1 tsp each sesame oil and sugar. Use on noodle salads, stir fries or steamed veggies.

GARLICKY YOGHURT DIP

Mix 1 cup Greek yoghurt, 1 grated garlic clove, juice of ½ lemon and a pinch of salt. Boom! Perfect with lamb, falafel or roast veggies.

HOW TO TOAST SPICES

Pop whole or ground spices in a dry pan and stir for 30–60 seconds until they smell fragrant and amazing. This wakes them up and makes food taste way fancier.

SCHEDULE A LEFTOVER NIGHT

Plan a weekly dinner that cleans out your fridge – think fried rice, pasta bakes and toasties.

Leftovers aren't second best, they're second chances!

FROZEN IS FABULOUS

Frozen veggies and fruit are just as good as fresh and usually cheaper, plus there's no chopping!

They're chill, they're cheap, and they're already chopped.

MEAT ONCE, EAT TWICE

Buy a bulk pack of meat and stretch it over two meals. Your fridge and wallet will thank you.

One tray of mince equals two dinners sorted.

DON'T SHOP ON AN EMPTY BELLY

Hungry shoppers buy snacks. Full shoppers buy dinner ingredients.

Step away from the snack aisle, you're just hangry!

HOW TO SAVE $$$ AT THE SHOPS

STICK TO THE LIST, QUEEN

Only write down what you actually need, and don't stray from the list.

Repeat after me: If it's not on the list, it's not going in the trolley.

START WITH THE FRESH STUFF

Cos they're cheaper, fill up on veggies first before your trolley gets distracted.

Shop like you're hungry for colour.

HOME-BRAND HEROES

There's no shame in going basic. It's often the same stuff as in the fancier box.

It's what's in the tin that counts.

READ THE SMALL NUMBERS

Check the price per 100g or kilo to spot the real bargains.

Tiny numbers tell big money stories.

BULK IT UP

Bigger bags of pantry staples like pasta, rice and oats give you more bang for your buck.

Think big now to save later.

BEND TO SAVE

The cheapest items in the supermarket are usually hiding on the bottom shelf.

Your wallet wins when you do a squat!

EASY WEEKEND WOW

—

Laid-back cooking that still brings the wow. These are the recipes for when you've got a little more time, want to treat your family or invite friends over, and still keep things simple. Big flavours, simple steps, and that little extra wow to make your weekend shine.

SERVES 8

This rich and hearty melt-in-your-mouth beef ragu is a total show-off dinner that's so easy! Just pop it the oven and forget about it until your house smells like an Italian trattoria and everyone's asking, 'What's for dinner?' And the best bit is it freezes like a treat for lazy dinner feeds.

RICH & READY BEEF RAGU

WHAT YOU NEED

- 1KG BEEF CHUCK STEAK, CUBED
- 1 TSP SALT
- 1 TSP PEPPER
- OLIVE OIL, TO DRIZZLE
- 2 ONIONS, DICED
- 2 CELERY STALKS, DICED
- 2 LARGE CARROTS, DICED
- 1 TBSP CRUSHED GARLIC
- 2 TBSP BEEF STOCK POWDER
- 2 BAY LEAVES
- 1 TBSP DRIED THYME
- 1 CUP RED WINE
- ½ CUP TOMATO PASTE
- 700ML JAR TOMATO PASSATA
- 1 BUNCH PARSLEY, LEAVES CHOPPED
- TO SERVE: PARMESAN CHEESE

WHAT YOU DO

Preheat your oven to 160°C.

Season your beef with the salt and pepper. Heat a drizzle of oil in a large oven-safe casserole over medium heat. Pop in half the beef – you will need to do this in two rounds so the beef browns, not steams. And let the underside turn golden before stirring. Throw in the onion, celery, carrot and garlic and cook for 5 minutes until they start to soften.

Now it's party time – add the beef stock powder, bay leaves, thyme, red wine, tomato paste, passata and 2 cups water to the pan. Stir it all together and let it bubble. Once the liquid is simmering, pop the lid on the pan and slide it into your oven for 2 hours.

Your will know the beef is perfectly cooked when it is so tender it can be pulled apart easily with a fork. Time to freshen things up. Stir the chopped parsley through the rich, saucy goodness and pull apart your beef. Serve with a big tangle of pasta – I love pappardelle or rigatoni to soak up all that ragu magic. Top with lots of parmesan and get ready for compliments!

PREP & COOK TIME

2½ hrs

BOSS BABE PULLED PORK

SERVES 6

Slow cooker pulled pork is the magical dinner that practically makes itself. You chuck everything in, walk away, and when you return, BOOM, you've got juicy, fall-apart pork packed with smoky, tangy flavour. Use for tacos, burgers, wraps or stuffing into baked spuds. Yum!

WHAT YOU NEED

40G PKT TACO SEASONING MIX (OR MAKE YOUR OWN, PAGE 84)

1 TBSP GROUND CUMIN

2 TSP SALT

2 TSP PEPPER

¼ CUP APPLE CIDER VINEGAR

¼ CUP BROWN SUGAR

1 THIN-SKINNED SEEDLESS ORANGE, HALVED

400G CAN DICED TOMATOES

1.5KG PIECE BONELESS PORK SHOULDER

WHAT YOU DO

Pop everything, except the pork and orange halves into a 5.5L (22-cup) slow cooker with 1 cup water. Give it a good whisk until the brown sugar dissolves into the mix, then add the orange halves.

Now, place your pork shoulder right into the middle and snuggle it down into the saucy goodness. Pop the lid on your slow cooker, set to LOW for 10 hours or HIGH for 6 hours.

Once it's done, give it 30-minute rest in the cooker to soak up even more flavour. Take the pork out and, using two forks, shred into tender strands. Toss out the orange halves, then pop the shredded pork back into the sauce. Give it a stir to coat every bit.

2 WAYS TO MAKE IT A MEAL

PULLED-PORK BURGERS
Fill brioche buns with slaw, the pulled pork and top with guacamole and Burger Sauce (page 94).

PULLED-PORK TACOS
Fill taco shells with the pulled pork and top with shredded lettuce, avocado, shredded cheese, sriracha and coriander leaves.

PREP & COOK TIME
LOW 10¼ hrs or HIGH 6¼ hrs

STEPH SAYS

NO AIR FRYER? NO WORRIES! JUST BAKE EVERYTHING IN THE OVEN FOR 15–20 MINUTES.

BUTTERED-UP PRAWNS & CHORIZO

SERVES 4

This recipe is a speedy flavour bomb – juicy prawns, smoky chorizo and buttery garlicky goodness, all done in the air fryer! This one's great as a starter with crusty bread to soak up all that sauce – or chuck it over some rice and salad for a knockout main.

WHAT YOU NEED

500G FROZEN PEELED GREEN PRAWNS (OPTIONAL: LEAVE TAILS INTACT)

2 TBSP OLIVE OIL

125G SALTED BUTTER, MELTED

1 TBSP CRUSHED GARLIC

1 TSP PEPPER

1 TSP SMOKED PAPRIKA

1 TSP GARLIC POWDER

1 TSP ONION POWDER

2 CURED CHORIZO, THINLY SLICED

TO SERVE: CRUSTY BREAD, LEMON AND PARSLEY

WHAT YOU DO

Pop your prawns into a colander and rinse under cold water to thaw. Pat the prawns dry with a paper towel so when they cook, they go golden, not soggy.

Remove the bottom tray of your air fryer – we're going to cook the prawns in the base among the saucy goodness. Pour in the olive oil and melted butter, then stir in your garlic and spices. Add the prawns and sliced chorizo. Give everything a good toss to coat in the buttery, garlicky spice mix.

Set the temperature to 200°C and the timer for 7 minutes, turning the prawns halfway through. You'll know they're done when your prawns are a lovely pink colour and the chorizo is crisp and golden. Scoop it all into bowls and serve with crusty bread, lemon and parsley. So yum.

PREP & COOK TIME
20 mins

CHEESEBURGER TACO PARTY

MAKES 8

Smash-burger tacos are what happens when a cheeseburger and a taco have a love child. These are fast, fun and full of juicy, cheesy goodness – just smash the hamburger mixture onto a tortilla and let the pan do the work.

WHAT YOU NEED

- 500G BEEF MINCE
- 1 TBSP SMOKED PAPRIKA
- 1 TSP ONION POWDER
- 1 TSP GARLIC POWDER
- 1 TSP PEPPER
- 2 TSP SALT
- 8 SMALL TORTILLAS
- 8 BURGER CHEESE SLICES
- 24 BREAD AND BUTTER PICKLES
- 1 CUP SHREDDED ICEBERG
- ½ ONION, DICED
- TO SERVE: MUSTARD AND TOMATO SAUCE (OPTIONAL)

FOR THE BURGER SAUCE

- ¼ CUP MAYONNAISE
- 2 TBSP TOMATO SAUCE
- 1 TBSP DIJON MUSTARD
- 3 BREAD AND BUTTER PICKLES, DICED
- 1 TBSP PICKLE JUICE

WHAT YOU DO

Let's make that epic burger sauce! Throw the sauce ingredients into a bowl and give it a good stir. Set aside – you'll want this on everything later.

Now, pop the beef mince into a bowl. Then, add the paprika, onion and garlic powders, pepper and salt. Get in there with your hands to mix everything until well combined. Divide the mix into eight mounds.

Lay out your tortillas on a bench. Then, top each with a mound of beef. Using your fingers or the back of spoon, flatten and spread the beef almost to the tortilla edge.

Heat your non-stick frying pan (or an electric frypan to cook multiples) over medium heat. Cook a tortilla, meat-side down, pressing down with a spatula. Let it sizzle away for 3 minutes or until the meat is golden. Flip the tortilla over, top with a cheese slice and cook for a further 2 minutes or until the tortilla is crisp and the cheese melts. Repeat until all your smash-burger tacos are cooked.

Now it's time to load 'em up! Smother with burger sauce, then with pickles, shredded lettuce and diced onion. Fold each in half like a taco and get munching.

PREP & COOK TIME
50 mins

STEPH SAYS

SHORT ON TIME? LEAVE THE DOUGH ON YOUR BENCH FOR 1–2 HOURS UNTIL DOUBLED, THEN ALLOW 30–60 MINUTES FOR THE SECOND RISE IN THE PAN.

SLUMBER-PARTY FOCACCIA

MAKES 1 LARGE LOAF

This soft, fluffy golden focaccia is a loaf of deliciousness that's begging to be dipped, dunked or customised with your favourite toppings for the best sandwich ever.

WHAT YOU NEED

4 CUPS PLAIN FLOUR

2 TSP SALT

1 TSP CASTER SUGAR

2 TSP DRIED YEAST (1 SACHET)

½ CUP OLIVE OIL

COOKING OIL SPRAY

OPTIONAL TOPPINGS

SEA SALT FLAKES

2 TBSP FRESH ROSEMARY LEAVES

½ CUP PITTED KALAMATA OLIVES

½ CUP SUN-DRIED TOMATOES

200G CHERRY TOMATOES, HALVED

WHAT YOU DO

In a large bowl, mix flour, yeast, salt and sugar. Make a well in the middle. Pour in 2 cups hot water. Using a spatula, mix until you've got a sticky dough. Drizzle over with 1½ tbsp oil. Using your fingers, gently rub the oil over the dough. Cover the bowl with plastic wrap and refrigerate overnight for a little beauty sleep.

The next day, spray a 20cm x 30cm baking pan with cooking oil and line with baking paper. Pour 1½ tbsp of the oil over the base of the pan. Spray your hands with oil so the dough doesn't stick. Give your dough a little punch in the middle.

Now, slide your fingers down one side of the bowl, lift the dough up and fold it into the middle. Give your bowl a quarter turn and do the same thing – repeat until you've gone all the way round and the dough is roughly ball-shaped.

Pop the dough into the oiled tray and turn to coat in oil, leave to rise at room temperature until doubled in size (2 hours if it's a warm day and up to 4 hours if cool).

Preheat your oven to 220°C.

Pour remaining ¼ cup olive oil over the dough. Using your fingertips, dimple the dough and gently press it toward the edges of the pan. Sprinkle with salt flakes and add toppings if you like – pressing them in gently.

Pop it in the oven for 30 minutes or until golden brown and smelling amazing. Cool for 10 minutes so it doesn't squish when you slice it.

Serve on its own or as a sandwich topped with mortadella, tomato, rocket, pesto, basil and bocconcini.

PREP & COOK TIME
35 mins (+ standing & overnight refrigeration)

SERVES 4, WITH LEFTOVERS

If you're after something sticky, glossy, savoury and a little bit fancy, this braised pork belly is your new best friend. It's sweet, salty and simple to throw together. The pork gets jammy and tender as it simmers away, soaking up a punchy sauce that'll have you licking the plate.

GLORIOUS GLOSSY PORK BELLY

WHAT YOU NEED

1 CUP NEUTRAL OIL

1KG PORK BELLY, CUT INTO 3CM PIECES

1 THUMB-SIZED PIECE GINGER, THINLY SLICED

6 CLOVES GARLIC, CRUSHED

3 STAR ANISE

2 BAY LEAVES

2 TBSP BROWN SUGAR

2 TBSP KECAP MANIS

2 TBSP SOY SAUCE

¼ CUP CHINESE COOKING WINE

TO SERVE: RICE, ASIAN GREENS AND SLICED GREEN ONION

WHAT YOU DO

Heat your oil in a large frying pan over medium heat. When it's hot, add the pork belly in a single layer and let it sizzle away for 5 minutes until golden on all sides. Scoop out the pork and ditch the oil (it's done its job).

Pop your ginger, garlic, star anise, bay leaves and brown sugar in the same pan. Give it a good stir until smelling amazing and the sugar is dissolved. Now, pour in the kecap manis, soy sauce and Chinese cooking wine and stir to mix together.

Tumble the golden pork belly back into the pan in and toss to coat in the glossy saucy goodness. Add just enough water to cover the pork, pop the lid on the pan, and bring it to a simmer.

Turn the heat down to low and simmer for 45 minutes or until the pork softens and soaks up all that yumminess.

Take the lid off and let it simmer for 10 minutes until the sauce is thick, shiny and coats the pork in a sticky glaze.

Serve with hot rice, some greens and sliced green onion for a no-stress dinner that tastes like it came from a fancy restaurant!

PREP & COOK TIME
1¼ hrs

SERVES 4

This is your one-pan ticket to flavour town! These Indian-style lamb shanks are slow-cooked until they're fall-apart tender in a rich, spiced tomato and onion gravy. Add some baby potatoes halfway through and let the oven do the rest!

BAKED & BRAISED BOLLYWOOD SHANKS

WHAT YOU NEED

- OLIVE OIL, TO DRIZZLE
- 4 ONIONS, SLICED
- 1 TSP SALT
- 1 TBSP CRUSHED GARLIC
- 1 TBSP CRUSHED GINGER
- 2 TSP GARAM MASALA
- 2 TSP GROUND CUMIN
- 1 TSP CHILLI POWDER
- 4 TOMATOES, DICED
- 1 TBSP CHICKEN STOCK POWDER
- 2 TBSP BALSAMIC VINEGAR
- 4 LAMB SHANKS
- 8 CHAT POTATOES
- TO SERVE: RICE, YOGHURT AND MINT LEAVES

WHAT YOU DO

Preheat your oven to 160°C.

Heat a large oven-safe casserole over medium heat with a drizzle of olive oil and add the onions. Let them sizzle for 10 minutes, giving them an occasional stir, so they don't turn crispy. Stir in your salt, garlic, ginger and all the gorgeous spices, and stir for 1 minute until it smells amazing.

Now, add your tomatoes, stock powder, balsamic vinegar and 2 cups water. Stir everything together until well combined. Nestle your lamb shanks in the mixture and bring to a simmer, then pop a lid on the pan.

Place the casserole in the oven and cook for 1½ hours. Time for the potato party! Flip your shanks over and toss in your potatoes. If the mixture is looking a bit dry, pour in 1 cup water so it stays saucy. Recover and pop it back in the oven for another hour or until the lamb is falling off the bone.

Serve the saucy shanks with some fluffy rice, a dollop of yoghurt, and mint leaves. Heaven.

PREP & COOK TIME
3 hrs

SERVES 4

This creamy salmon pasta is a total show-off dinner that's secretly easy – you'll feel like a kitchen superstar! It's zesty, silky, and packed with flavour – whether you're using fresh salmon or a handy can, this dish is yum with zero stress.

LAZY LUXE SALMON FETTUCCINE

WHAT YOU NEED

500G DRIED FETTUCCINE

OLIVE OIL, TO DRIZZLE

2 SKINLESS SALMON FILLETS OR 400G CAN PINK SALMON, DRAINED AND FLAKED

1 TBSP CRUSHED GARLIC

½ CUP WHITE WINE

300ML THICKENED CREAM

1 LEMON, ZEST AND JUICE

1 TBSP CHICKEN STOCK POWDER

300G SPINACH LEAVES

2 TBSP CAPERS

1 TSP CRACKED PEPPER

WHAT YOU DO

Boil your fettuccine in a large pot of salty water following the packet instructions. Scoop out ¼ cup pasta water, then drain.

While that's cooking, heat a drizzle of olive oil in frying pan over medium heat. Add your fresh salmon fillets and cook for 4 minutes on each side or until just cooked through, then set aside.

In the same pan, add the garlic and give it a quick stir for 30 seconds – don't let it burn! Pour in the white wine, cream, lemon zest and stock powder. Whisk together until it starts bubbling, then turn the heat down to low. Let it bubble gently for 5 minutes until thicker and yummy. If you're using canned salmon, add it now and stir through the sauce.

Now, toss in the spinach, capers, cracked pepper, cooked pasta and a splash of the pasta water you saved. Using salad servers or tongs, gently toss together so the pasta is coated.

Divide the pasta among bowls and flake the cooked salmon over the top. Finish with lemon juice, scatter with parsley and you're done!

PREP & COOK TIME
20 mins

STEPH SAYS

WANT A LITTLE HERBY FRESHNESS? TRY A HANDFUL OF PARSLEY LEAVES OR DILL SPRIGS. VOILÀ!

SERVES 6, WITH LEFTOVERS

This one's low-and-slow green goodness, and secretly a total breeze. Fall-apart lamb, oven-roasted to perfection, with a punchy chimichurri sauce that does all the heavy lifting in the flavour department. It's one of those dinners that makes you look fancy without even trying!

SHOW-STOPPING LAMB SHOULDER

WHAT YOU NEED

- 1 BIG BUNCH PARSLEY
- 4 CLOVES GARLIC
- 1 SMALL CHILLI
- ⅓ CUP RED WINE VINEGAR
- 1 CUP OLIVE OIL
- ½ TSP EACH SALT AND PEPPER
- 2KG LAMB SHOULDER WITH BONE

WHAT YOU DO

Preheat your oven to 160°C.

Let's start making the chimichurri. Strip leaves and tender stems from parsley, and pop them into a food processor with garlic, chilli, vinegar, oil and salt and pepper. Blitz until chopped up and saucy – I like mine a bit chunky! Set half the sauce aside for serving.

Next, put your lamb into a baking dish and pour over the rest of the sauce. Get in there with your hands and rub the sauce over the lamb so it's coated in herby goodness. Pour 2 cups water around the lamb without wetting it, then cover the dish tightly with two layers of foil.

Pop it in the oven for 3 hours. Go put your feet up – your lamb is doing all the work.

After 3 hours, remove the foil and turn the oven up to 220°C. Return to the oven for a further 20 minutes or until golden and sizzled and meat is starting to fall off the bone.

To serve it up, shred the meat with two forks and enjoy with your reserved chimichurri.

PREP & COOK TIME
3½ hrs

SWEET & SIMPLE
—

Desserts that deliver without the drama. These easy treats are big on comfort and low on effort – think quick puddings, no-fuss bakes and sweet little wins for any night of the week. Let's dive into the delicious end of dinner!

SERVES 4

This classic chocolate pudding is what cosy dreams are made of. It's rich, gooey, and magically makes its own chocolate sauce while it bakes! You mix it, pour it, bake it – and voilà! Dessert magic in under an hour.

HOT MESS CHOC DESSERT

WHAT YOU NEED

½ CUP MILK

1 EGG

100G MELTED BUTTER

1 CUP SELF-RAISING FLOUR

¼ CUP COCOA POWDER

½ CUP BROWN SUGAR

TO SERVE: VANILLA ICE-CREAM

FOR THE CHOC SAUCE

2 TBSP COCOA POWDER

¾ CUP BROWN SUGAR

WHAT YOU DO

Preheat your oven to 180°C.

Pop your milk, egg and melted butter into a large bowl and whisk it together like a champ. Add the flour, cocoa and brown sugar and stir until it's smooth and thick (no lumps allowed!).

Grease a 1.5 litre baking dish and pour in the batter. Go on, give the bowl a little lick.

Now for the saucy bit! Mix the cocoa and brown sugar in a small bowl and sprinkle it evenly over your batter.

Grab a large metal spoon and hold it upside down just above the batter. Gently pour 1¼ cup boiling water over the back of the spoon – it'll look strange now but trust the process!

Carefully pop your dish into the oven and bake for 35 minutes until the top looks set and underneath is bubbling away like a hot, chocolatey swamp.

Serve it up while it's warm with a big scoop of vanilla ice-cream. Heaven!

PREP & COOK TIME
45 mins

SERVES 4

These dumplings are the ultimate old-school comfort treat – soft, warm and swimming in a rich, sticky sauce. This stove top recipe is so easy you just need a pan, a lid, and a little patience. Perfect for chilly nights or sweet cravings, this one's a keeper!

SAUCY GOLDEN SYRUP DUMPLING DREAMS

WHAT YOU NEED

1½ CUPS SELF-RAISING FLOUR

1 CUP GREEK YOGHURT

PINCH OF SALT

TO SERVE: ICE-CREAM

FOR THE BROWN SUGAR SYRUP

½ CUP BROWN SUGAR

½ CUP GOLDEN SYRUP

50G BUTTER

1 TSP SALT

WHAT YOU DO

Let's start with the brown sugar syrup. Grab a large pan with a lid and pop in the brown sugar, golden syrup, butter, salt and 2 cups water. Bring the sweet mixture to the boil over medium heat – it will smell amazing!

While it's bubbling away, get started on the dumplings: mix the flour, yoghurt and pinch of salt in a bowl until a soft, squishy dough forms. Break the dough off into meatball-sized chunks (just use your hands – no fancy rolling here!).

Drop the dumplings gently into the sauce – being careful not to splash! Pop the lid on, turn the heat down to low, and let the magic happen for 20 minutes. No peeking – seriously!

When the time's up, lift the lid and get ready for some fluffy golden clouds floating in sticky syrupy goodness. Serve with your favourite ice-cream.

PREP & COOK TIME
40 mins

STEPH SAYS

DON'T FORGET TO SMOTHER THEM IN CREAM OR ICE-CREAM FOR THE ULTIMATE SWEET TREAT!

STEPH SAYS

EAT WARM WITH ICE-CREAM OR STRAIGHT-UP USING YOUR HANDS – NO JUDGEMENT HERE!

MAKES 18

Sometimes, all you need is a cookie to turn your day around. This one is packed with melty choc chips and a little sprinkle of salty magic for a sweet-salty hit. No fancy gear needed – just mix, bake and try not to eat the whole lot in one go!

CHEWY CHOCCY COOKIE BARS

WHAT YOU NEED

200G BUTTER, CHOPPED

1 CUP BROWN SUGAR

½ CUP CASTER SUGAR

2 EGGS

1 TSP VANILLA EXTRACT

2½ CUPS PLAIN FLOUR

1 TSP BAKING POWDER

250G DARK OR MILK CHOCOLATE CHIPS

2 TSP SALT FLAKES (OPTIONAL)

WHAT YOU DO

Preheat your oven to 160°C.

Melt your butter in a large microwave-safe bowl on LOW in 10-second bursts. Add both sugars and whisk until smooth and glossy. Crack in the eggs, then add the vanilla. Give it another good whisk to combine.

Now, add the flour and baking powder and stir until almost combined. Then, scatter over the choccy chips and stir until you've got a thick, cookie dough party going on.

Line a 20cm x 30cm slice pan with baking paper, extending the paper 5cm over edges. Press your dough in smoothly and evenly. Sprinkle with salt flakes if you're feeling fancy.

Bake the slab for 25 minutes or until it's golden and smells like heaven. Let it cool in the pan for 15 minutes (if you can wait that long!), then slice into 18 chunky slabs.

PREP & COOK TIME
40 mins

MAKES ABOUT 2 CUPS

Sweet, zingy, and totally dreamy, this lemon curd is like sunshine in a jar. Dollop it on scones, swirl it through cream, pour it over ice-cream, or sneak a spoonful straight from the fridge (I won't tell!). And the best part, it's made in the microwave, so no standing over the stove.

SUNSHINE IN A JAR

WHAT YOU NEED

125G BUTTER, CHOPPED

1 CUP CASTER SUGAR

1 CUP LEMON JUICE

ZEST OF 2 LEMONS

3 EGGS

WHAT YOU DO

First, get your jars squeaky clean by running them through the dishwasher so they are ready to fill.

Melt your butter into a large microwave-safe bowl on LOW in 10-second bursts. Add the sugar, lemon juice, and zest to the bowl and give it a good whisk to combine. Crack in the eggs and whisk again until everything is smooth and happy.

Microwave the lemony mixture for 1 minute, then whisk until smooth. Repeat alternating microwaving and whisking for 3–5 minutes or until thickened. You'll know it's ready when you dip a spoon in, run your finger down the back, and the curd stays put instead of running back together.

Just a word of caution, take care not to overheat the mixture, or it will split. If this starts to happen, quickly place the bowl over a second filled with iced water and whisk for your life to cool it and bring it back together.

Carefully pour the hot curd into the clean jars, pop the lids on and refrigerate for up to 2 weeks, using a clean spoon each time you scoop.

Try on scones, toast, pancakes, meringue nests, between cake layers, folded though whipped cream and drizzled over ice-cream … or in a Pucker Up Mug Cake (page 118).

PREP & COOK TIME
20 mins

MANGO WIGGLE AND WHIRL

MAKES 4, WITH LEFTOVERS

Get ready for a summer dessert that's fruity, fun and vibrant! This mango falooda is a chilled, layered Indian-style sweet treat with jelly, noodles, homemade mango sorbet and cream for something that looks fancy but is a breeze to put together.

WHAT YOU NEED

85G PKT MANGO JELLY CRYSTALS

500G FROZEN MANGO PIECES

JUICE OF 1 LIME

JUICE OF 2 LARGE ORANGES

1 TSP GROUND CARDAMOM

½ CUP SLIVERED ALMONDS

100G DRIED RICE VERMICELLI NOODLES

POURING CREAM

WHAT YOU DO

First make the mango jelly following the packet instructions. Grab your fanciest parfait bowl or individual glasses (really, any bowl or glasses will do). Pour in the jelly then refrigerate for 4 hours to set.

In a food processor, blitz the frozen mango, lime juice, orange juice and cardamom until smooth, like a thick smoothie. Scoop the mango mixture into a container and freeze for 3 hours or until firm – you've just made the easiest mango sorbet!

Preheat your oven to 180°C. Place the almonds on an oven tray and toast for 5 minutes or until golden and fragrant, then set aside to cool.

Cook the vermicelli noodles in a pan of boiling water following the instructions on the packet, drain, then pop them aside to cool.

To serve, top mango jelly with the cooled vermicelli noodles and generous scoops of mango sorbet. Finish with a drizzle of cream for a swirl of richness and a scattering of crunchy toasted almonds.

PREP & COOK TIME

20 mins (+ chilling & freezing)

SWEET TOOTH EMERGENCY: MIDNIGHT MUG CAKES

JAMMY DODGERS MUG CAKE

Microwave 20g butter in a big mug for 10-ish seconds to melt. Tip butter into a bowl. Whisk in 2 tbsp milk, followed by 2 tbsp caster sugar, 1 tsp vanilla extract, then 1 egg. Add ⅓ cup self-raising flour and a pinch of baking soda. Whisk until combined. Pour half the mixture into the same mug. Then, add 2 tbsp berry jam of choice in the middle. Top with remaining batter. Continue with microwave instructions above.

Serve with custard.

PUCKER UP MUG CAKE

Microwave 20g butter in a big mug for 10-ish seconds to melt. Tip butter into a bowl. Whisk in 2 tbsp milk, followed by 2 tbsp caster sugar, zest of ½ lemon, then 1 egg. Add ⅓ cup self-raising flour, and a pinch of baking soda. Whisk until combined. Pour half the mixture into the same mug. Then, add 2 tbsp Sunshine in a Jar (page 114) in the middle. Top with remaining batter. Continue with microwave instructions above.

Serve with extra lemon curd and vanilla ice-cream.

MAKES 1

Microwave mug cake for 75–90 seconds – keeping an eye on it after 60 seconds. Once it rises, it's ready! Let it cool for a minute or two (if you can wait), so you don't burn your tongue.

PREP & COOK TIME 5 mins

BUZZIN' BISCOFF MUG CAKE

Microwave 20g butter in a big mug for 10-ish seconds to melt. Tip butter into a bowl. Stir in ½ tsp instant coffee powder until dissolved. Tip into a bowl. Whisk in 2 tbsp milk, 2 tbsp brown sugar, followed by 1 egg. Add ⅓ cup self-raising flour and a pinch of baking soda. Whisk until lusciously smooth. Pour half the mixture into the same mug. Then add 2 tbsp Biscoff spread in the middle. Top with remaining batter. Continue with microwave instructions above.

Serve dusted with icing sugar.

GOOEY CHOC-IN-A-MUG

Microwave 20g butter in a big mug for 10-ish seconds to melt. Tip butter into a bowl. Whisk in 2 tbsp milk, followed by 2 tbsp brown sugar, then 1 egg. Add 2 tbsp self-raising flour, 2 tbsp cocoa, and a pinch of baking soda. Whisk until chocolatey and delish. Pour half the deliciousness into the same mug. Then, add 2 tbsp Nutella in the middle. Top with remaining deliciousness. Continue with microwave instructions above.

Serve with a dollop of double cream.

CRUMBLE-A-LICIOUS PEAR MAGIC

SERVES 4

There's something irresistible about a cosy fruit crumble. And this one's no fuss, all flavour, and totally dreamy. Fresh or canned pears meet warming spices and a crown of golden, coconutty topping that's crunchy in all the right places.

WHAT YOU NEED

- 825G CANNED PEAR SLICES IN SYRUP OR 1KG FRESH PEARS
- ¼ CUP CASTER SUGAR (IF USING FRESH PEARS)
- 2 TSP GROUND GINGER
- 1 TSP GARAM MASALA
- 1 TBSP CORNFLOUR
- 1 CUP PLAIN FLOUR
- 1 CUP SHREDDED COCONUT
- 1 CUP ROLLED OATS
- 1 CUP BROWN SUGAR
- 125G BUTTER, MELTED
- TO SERVE: CREAM, CUSTARD OR ICE-CREAM

WHAT YOU DO

If you're using fresh pears, peel, core and cut into thin wedges. Pop in a microwave-safe bowl with the caster sugar and ½ cup water. Cover with a dinner plate and microwave on HIGH for 5 minutes or until just tender.

Now, grab a 20cm square baking dish. Add the freshly cooked pears and syrup (or canned pears with the syrup) to the baking dish. Sprinkle over the ginger, garam masala and cornflour, and give it a gentle stir to combine the warm, spiced flavours.

Preheat your oven to 180°C or air fryer to 160°C.

In a big bowl, add your flour, coconut, oats and brown sugar. Pour over the melted butter and mix with a wooden spoon until you have a crumbly delicious topping.

Grab a handful of the crumble mix, squeeze it gently to form clumps, then arrange it over the top of the pears. This gives you those big, chunky, golden bits everyone loves.

Pop the pear crumble in the oven for 25 minutes or air fryer for 18 minutes or until the top is golden and smelling like dessert heaven.

Serve it warm with cream, custard or big scoops of vanilla ice-cream (or all three – I never saw anything!).

PREP & COOK TIME
40 mins

STEPH SAYS

TOP WITH SOME FRESH BERRIES AND A BIG SCOOP OF DOUBLE CREAM.

SERVES 4, WITH LEFTOVERS

This no-bake berry beauty is the ultimate make-ahead dessert! Summer pudding is a colourful, squishy, fruity dream made with layers of juicy berries and soft bread that soaks up all the goodness. It's sweet, a little tart and absolutely delightful with a dollop of cream on top.

SUMMER BERRY BOMBSHELL PUDDING

WHAT YOU NEED

1KG MIXED BERRIES (FROZEN IS FINE)

½ CUP CASTER SUGAR

½ TSP GROUND STAR ANISE (OPTIONAL)

12–15 SLICES OF THIN WHITE BREAD

TO SERVE: EXTRA MIXED BERRIES AND DOUBLE CREAM (OPTIONAL)

WHAT YOU DO

Pop your berries, sugar, star anise and ¼ cup water into a pan and bring to the boil over medium heat. Let it bubble away for 5 minutes until the sugar dissolves. Set aside to cool.

Line a 1-litre bowl with plastic wrap, leaving some hanging over the side – you'll use this later to wrap the top.

Trim the crusts off your bread slices. Start by placing a slice in the base of your bowl then, using more slices, line the side, slightly overlapping each one so there are no gaps. Leave about 2cm at the top without bread.

Strain the cooked berries but keep the juice! Spoon the berries into your bread-lined bowl. Now, gently spoon the juice over the berries and the edges of the bread to help it all soak in.

Cover the top with more bread slices to completely seal. Fold the plastic wrap in to tightly cover and seal.

Place the pudding on a small tray, then cover the top with a small plate and weight with something heavy like a couple of cans to press down. Pop in the fridge for at least 24 hours – or up to 3 days, if you're ahead of the game.

When you're ready to serve, remove the weight and plate. Flip the bowl onto a serving plate, lift off the bowl and peel away the wrapping.

PREP & COOK TIME

20 mins (+ cooling and overnight refrigeration)

NO STRESS PANTRY ESSENTIALS

GROUPED INTO CATEGORIES SO IT'S SUPER EASY TO STOCK UP AND KEEP ON HAND, THIS LIST CONTAINS YOUR GO-TO HEROES THAT REPEAT ACROSS MY RECIPES AND WILL KEEP YOU COOKING.

SAUCES & CONDIMENTS

- Soy sauce
- Oyster sauce
- Kecap manis
- Fish sauce
- Sweet chilli sauce
- Tomato paste
- Cooking oils (olive and vegetable)
- Cooking wine (Chinese or dry white wine)
- Vinegar (red, white and rice wine)

SPICES & SEASONINGS

- Stock powder (beef, chicken and veggie)
- Curry powder
- Garam masala
- Ground cumin
- Chilli powder
- Dried oregano
- Ground nutmeg
- Salt and pepper
- Sugar (white and brown)

FLAVOUR BOOSTERS

- Crushed garlic (jarred or fresh)
- Crushed ginger (jarred or fresh)
- Honey
- Lime or lemon juice (bottled or fresh)
- Cornflour

FREEZER FAVOURITES

- Peeled prawns
- Bao buns and dumplings
- Fruit (berries, mango, etc.)
- Veggies (peas, spinach, corn and carrot mix, etc.)

CANS OF CONVENIENCE

- Coconut milk
- Tomatoes
- Chickpeas
- Baby prawns
- Beans (kidney or black)

GRAINS & CARBS

- Pasta (penne, rigatoni, macaroni and fettuccine)
- Noodles (vermicelli, Hokkien, etc.)
- Rice
- Red split lentils
- Couscous

SNACKY ADD-INS & GARNISHES

- Crispy noodles
- Peanuts

CONVERSION CHART

REGIONAL VARIATIONS

One Australian teaspoon holds 5ml, one Australian tablespoon holds 20ml, one Australian cup holds 250ml. Measuring cups differ between countries but the variation should not affect your cooking results. North America, New Zealand and the United Kingdom use a 15ml tablespoon, so if you are using a tablespoon manufactured for one of these countries, use 3 teaspoons to measure each tablespoon instead. All cup and spoon measurements used are level.

All eggs used are an average of 60g each.

All oven temperatures used are fan-forced. If you are using a conventional oven, increase the recommended temperature by 10–20 degrees.

Measurements for baking dishes and pans are approximate only. Using a similarly shaped pan of a similar size should not affect your baking results.

DRY AND LIQUID MEASURES

Metric	Imperial
5g / 5ml	⅛ oz / ⅛ fluid oz
15g / 15ml	½oz / ½ fluid oz
30g / 30ml	1oz / 1 fluid oz
60g / 60ml	2oz / 2 fluid oz
90g / 90ml	3oz / 3 fluid oz
125g / 125ml	4oz (¼ lbs) / 4 fluid oz
250g / 250ml	8oz (½ lbs) / 8 fluid oz
500g / 500ml	16oz (1 lbs) / 16 fluid oz
1kg / 1 litre	32oz (2 lbs) / 1¾ pints

LENGTH MEASURES

Metric	Imperial
2cm	¾ inch
3cm	1¼ inches
4cm	1½ inches
5cm	2 inches
16cm	6 inches
20cm	8 inches
30cm	12 inches (1 foot)

OVEN TEMPERATURES

Celsius	Fahrenheit
75°C	170°F
160°C	320°F
180°C	350°F
200°C	400°F
220°C	430°F

THANK YOU TO MY SPONSORS

gorman

KIP&CO

CRUMBLE

INDEX

A

apple & pork sizzle up 55

B

bachelor's handbag dinner hacks 70
baked & braised Bollywood shanks 101
bao buns, sticky pork belly 37
beef
    & chickpeas, Moroccan 60
    mince magic rice bowl 20
    noodle salad, Thai 24
    ragu 89
    stroganoff 63
berry pudding 123
big-batch Tex-Mex chilli 79
Bolognese, boss-level 76
boss babe pulled pork 90
boss-level Bolognese 76
bread, focaccia 97
broccoli, chicken mornay 80
brown sugar syrup 110
burger
    pulled pork 90
    sauce 94
    taco party 94
butter chook spice mix 84
buttered-up prawns & chorizo 93
buzzin' Biscoff mug cake 119

C

cheat's chicken biryani 75
cheeseburger taco party 94
chewy choccy cookie bars 113
chicken
    biryani, cheat's 75
    & cheese chimichangas 71
    Chinese-style 52
    green goodness mac attack 19
    mornay 80
    Moroccan tray bake 48
    & mushroom risotto 74
    noodle soup 72
    parcel party packs 43
    perfect roast 66
    salad or sandwich 73
    Spanish-style 61
    tikka masala 59
chilli, Tex-Mex 79
chimichangas, chicken & cheese 71
chimichurri 105
Chinese-style marinade 67
choc sauce 109
chocolate cookie bars 113
chocolate dessert 109
chorizo & prawns 93
coconut curry fish 16
cookie bars, chewy choccy 113
coriander yoghurt sauce 48
cosy curry sauce dumplings 47
creamy chicken mornay magic 80
crispy potato dinner bombs 44
crumble-a-licious pear magic 120
curry
    chicken tikka masala 59
    coconut fish 16
    super speedy dippy dahl 31
curry paste, basic 84
curry sauce dumplings 47

D

dahl, super speedy 31
dip, garlicky yoghurt 84
dressings & sauces (savoury)
    Asian 84
    burger 94
    chimichurri 105
    coriander yoghurt 48
    garlicky yoghurt 7
    go-to salad 7
    sang choi bau 28
    sticky pork 37
    stir-fry 7
    Thai 24
    zingy 27
dressings & sauces (sweet), chocolate 109
dumplings
    cosy curry sauce 47
    golden syrup 110

E

easy Asian dressing 84
easy chicken & mushroom risotto 74

F

fast & sassy Thai beef noodle salad 24
fish
    coconut curry 16
    one-tray miso salmon 51
    salmon fettuccine 102
focaccia 97
freezer stash mash 83
fried rice
    mince magic 20
    sticky pork belly 41

G

garlicky yoghurt 7
garlicky yoghurt dip 84
glorious glossy pork belly 98
golden noodle stir-up 12
golden sausage pasta magic 32
golden syrup dumplings 110
gooey choc-in-a-mug 119
grapes, Chinese-style chicken 52
green goodness mac attack 19

H

hot mess choc dessert 109

I

Indian-style marinade 67

J

jammy dodgers mug cake 118

K

Korean-style marinade 67

L

laksa that loves you back 23
lamb
    chops, souvlaki-style 7
    ragu 62
    shanks, Indian-style 101
    shoulder, show-stopping 105
    tray bake 56
lasagne, Tex-Mex chilli 79
lazy luxe salmon fettuccine 102
lemon curd 114

M

mango wiggle and whirl 117
marinades
    Chinese-style 67
    Indian-style 67
    Korean-style 67
    Moroccan-style 67
    Steph's spicy fave 67
    sweet & sticky 84

mashed potato 83
mince magic rice bowl 20
mince, cooking tip 7
miso, one-tray salmon 51
Moroccan beef and chickpeas 60
Moroccan chicken magic tray bake 48
Moroccan-style marinade 67
mug cakes
    chocolate 119
    cookie butter 119
    jam 118
    lemon 118
mushroom & chicken risotto 74

N

nachos, Tex-Mex chilli 79
noodle
    chicken soup 72
    & pork slurp-up 27
    pork stir-fry 12
    prawn laksa 23
    sticky pork belly stir-fry 38
no-stress taco seasoning 84

O

one-pan coconut curry fish delight 16
one-tray miso salmon miracle 51
onions, sautéing 7

P

pasta
    beef ragu 89
    Bolognese 76
    cooking tip 7
    golden sausage magic 32
    green goodness macaroni 19
    ravioli with tomato and basil 15
    salmon fettuccine 102
pear crumble 120
perfect roast chicken 66
pork
    & apple sizzle up 55
    golden noodle stir-up 12
    noodle slurp-up 27
    pulled 90
    sang choi bau 28
pork belly
    glossy 98
    sticky bites 37

potato
    baked dinner bombs 44
    mash 83
    Tex-Mex chilli 79
prawn laksa 23
prawns & chorizo 93
pucker up mug cake 118
puddings
    chocolate 109
    summer berry 123

Q

quick chicken noodle soup 72

R

ravioli with tomato and basil magic 15
rice
    chicken biryani 75
    cooking tip 7
rice bowl
    mince magic 20
    sticky pork belly 40
rich & ready beef ragu 89
risoni, Tex-Mex chilli 79
risotto, chicken & mushroom 74
roast chicken meets Chinatown 52

S

salad
    chicken 73
    sticky pork belly 39
sandwich, chicken salad 73
sang choi bau sauce 28
sang choi bau wow! 28
saucy golden syrup dumpling dreams 110
saucy pork & noodle slurp-up 27
sausage, golden pasta magic 32
show-stopping lamb shoulder 105
sizzle & drizzle lamb chops souvlaki-style 7
sizzle up pork & apple 55
slammin' lamb tray bake 56
slow cooker dump bag dream dinners 58
slumber-party focaccia 97
soup, chicken noodle 72
souvlaki-style lamb chops 7
Spanish-style chicken 61

spice mix
    butter chicken 84
    Greek blend 84
    Steph's sprinkle 84
    taco 84
    toasting 84
Steph's lazy-girl Greek blend 84
Steph's spicy fave marinade 67
Steph's sprinkle 84
sticky pork belly
    Asian salad 39
    bao buns 37
    bites 37
    fried rice 41
    noodle stir-fry 38
    rice bowls 40
sticky sauce 37
stir fry
    pork & noodle 27
    golden noodle 12
    sticky pork belly noodle 38
summer berry bombshell pudding 123
sunshine in a jar 114
super speedy dippy dahl 31
sweet & sticky marinade 84
syrup, brown sugar 110

T

taco
    cheeseburger 94
    pulled pork 90
    Tex-Mex chilli 79
Thai dressing 24
the best basic curry paste 84
the best chicken salad or sandwich 73
tomato and basil ravioli 15

V

vegetables, roasting tip 7

Y

yoghurt
    garlicky 7
    garlicky dip 84

Z

zingy sauce 27

HarperCollinsPublishers
Australia • Brazil • Canada • France • Germany
Holland • India • Italy • Japan • Mexico • New Zealand
Poland • Spain • Sweden • Switzerland
United Kingdom • United States of America

HarperCollins acknowledges the Traditional Custodians of the lands upon which we live and work, and pays respect to Elders past and present.

First published on Gadigal Country in Australia in 2026 by HarperCollins*Publishers* Australia Pty Limited
ABN 36 009 913 517
harpercollins.com.au

Copyright © Steph Cooks Stuff Pty Ltd 2026

The right of Steph de Sousa to be identified as the author of this work has been asserted by her in accordance with the *Copyright Act 1968*.

All rights reserved. Apart from any use as permitted under the *Copyright Act 1968*, no part may be reproduced, copied, scanned, stored in a retrieval system, recorded, or transmitted, in any form or by any means, without the prior written permission of the publisher. Without limiting the exclusive rights of any author, contributor, or the publisher of this publication, any unauthorised use of this publication to train generative artificial intelligence (AI) technologies is expressly prohibited. HarperCollins also exercises its rights under Article 4(3) of the Digital Single Market Directive 2019/790 and expressly reserves this publication from the text and data-mining exception.

HarperCollinsPublishers
Macken House, 39/40 Mayor Street Upper
Dublin 1, D01 C9W8, Ireland

A catalogue record for this book is available from the National Library of Australia

ISBN 978 1 4607 6873 0 (paperback)
ISBN 978 1 4607 1934 3 (ebook)

Publisher: Roberta Ivers
Project editor: Shannon Kelly
Food editor: Sophia Young
Proofreader: Libby Turner
Stylist: Olivia Blackmore
Photochef: Rebecca Lyall
Hair and make-up: Allison Boyle
Cover and internal design by Mietta Yans, HarperCollins Design Studio
Cover and internal photography by Alana Landsberry
Index by Shannon Kelly
Colour reproduction by Splitting Image Colour Studio, Wantirna, Victoria
Printed and bound in China

8 7 6 5 4 3 2 1   26 27 28 29 30